Tobias Mattes

The abuse of mass media by international terrorist organizations

The online magazine "Rumiyah" and the propaganda of the Islamic State

D1739924

Bibliografische Information der Deutschen Nationalbibliothek:

Die Deutsche Nationalbibliothek verzeichnet diese Publikation in der Deutschen Nationalbibliografie; detaillierte bibliografische Daten sind im Internet über http://dnb.d-nb.de abrufbar.

Impressum:

Copyright © Studylab 2019

Ein Imprint der Open Publishing GmbH, München

Druck und Bindung: Books on Demand GmbH, Norderstedt, Germany

Coverbild: Open Publishing GmbH | Freepik.com | Flaticon.com | ei8htz

Table of Contents

Abstract

This master thesis purposes to provide a qualitative content analyses of *"Rumi-yah"*, the monthly magazine published by Al Hayat Media Center, the official Media Department of the Islamic State. For this research 13 issues of the magazine will be examined from 1st publication on September 5th2016 to the 13th publication on September 9th2017. The main aim of this paper is to identify the kind of used triggers in the magazine, that can promote radicalization. In the run-up to the presentation of the analysis results, the current state of the scientific findings about radicalization research is introduced. The results of the content analysis will be compared with the results of analogous studies on the *"Dabiq"* magazine, before possible counter measures will be suggested and how they can be put into the practice. The main objective of the study is to understand the messages propagated through this magazine and how this knowledge can be used from governmental agencies to build up a functional counter-strategy against Islamic State's radicalization attempts in online jihad.

List of Abbreviations

BfV	Federal Office for the Protection of the Constitution
BKA	Federal Office for Criminal Investigations
BLKA	Bavarian State Office of Criminal Investigations
BMI	Federal Ministry of the Interior
BND	Federal Intelligence Service
DAESH	ad-daula al islāmiyya fī l-'Irāq wa-š-Šām (acronym of Arabic name)
EU	European Union
IMAG	Intra-ministerial working group (in context of the center for deradicalization of the Bavarian police)
IS	Islamic State
ISD	Institute for Strategic Dialogue
ISI	Islamic State of Iraq
ISIL	Islamic State of the Iraq and the Levante
ISIS	Islamic State of Syria
N.N.	Nomen nominandum
NGO	Non-Governmental Organizations
PKS	Police Crime Statistics
PMAK	Politically motivated foreign crime
UN	United Nations
VPN	Violence Prevention Network

List of Figures

The Islamic Glossary

Alhamdulillah	engl.: thank god
Amirul-Mu'minin	leader of the faithful (Muslims)
'Aqīdah	the matters and fundamental foundations known from the Koran and the hadith, to which Muslims must confidently and with conviction believe with heart and mind
Bayʿa, pl.: Bayʿāt	oath of allegiance to a leader
Bayt al-Maqdis	Jerusalem (literally: holy city)
Dabiq	a place in northern Syria called an Armageddon Hadith, where, according to the IS interpretation, the end-time battle between Muslims and unbelievers will take place after the apocalypse begins; Magazine of the IS, which is named after this place
Dar al-Kufr	area of unbelief (as opposed to Dar al-Islam)
Da'wah	"call to Islam" in the sense of missionary activity
Duʿā'	prayer, supplication
Hadith, pl.: Ahadith	(single) transmission of the saying, action, approval or characteristics of Muhammad
hafidhahullāh	engl.: May Allah preserve him (in good)
Hijrah	originally Muhammad's emigration from Mecca to Medina; in the IS propaganda: emigration to the caliphate (i.e. emigration to IS-area)
Imārah	emirate
Inghimāsi	"Honorary title" of IS for suicide bombers
Istishhādi, pl.:Istishhādiyyīn	martyr
Jama`ah	community
Jāhiliyyah	Time of ancient Arab paganism before Islam
Jawlānī-Front	Al-Nusra Front (since 28.07.2016: Jabhat Fatah Al-Sham), a jihadist-salafist group in Syria, which until its renaming belonged to al Qaeda and was classified by the United Nations as a terrorist organization

Jihad	struggle, effort, commitment in the way of Allah; holy war
Jumu'ah	friday's prayer of the Muslims
Kāfir, pl.: Kāfirūn/Kuffār	disbeliever, godless one
Khalīfah	caliph
Khilāfah	caliphate
Kufr	disbelieve
kufrī	adjective to Kufr: disbelieving
Manhaj	to obtain, analyze and implement method or methodology (religious) knowledge (mostly from Koran and Sunnah)
Mujāhid, fem.: Mujāhidah, pl.: Mujāhidūn/ Mujāhidīn	for the faith (in jihad)
Murtad, pl.: Murtaddīn	apostate (someone who has fallen from Islam)
Mushrik, pl.: Mushrikūn/ Mushrikīn	polytheist, idol worshiper
Muwahhid, pl.: Muwahhidūn/Muwahhidīn	confessor of the unity of god, monotheist
Radiyallahu 'anhum	engl.: Allah's pleasure in them
Rāfidah	designation of those who reject legitimate Islamic authority and leadership from the point of view of the person using the term
Rahimahullāh	engl: may god have mercy on him
Rasulullah	messenger of god (Muhammad)
Salaf	the righteous ancestors / ancestors (in Islam), mostly the first three generations of Muslims
(al-) Shām	Syria (sometimes also other surrounding areas locked in)
Sharī'ah or. sharia	religious law of Islam
Shaykh	honorable title in Arabic, e.g. for tribal leaders or important Islamic clerics
Shirk	unbelief on the basis of an assertion of another to the uniqueness and oneness of god, that is, polytheism and idolatry; Often, the Christian doctrine of the trinity is called shirk

shirkī	adjective to Shirk: polytheistic, blasphemous, idolatrous
subhanahu	praise to him
Sunnah	acts of the Prophet, thus exemplary and imitative behavior, also commands and recommendations of Muhammad (basis of the Sunnah are the hadiths)
Tāghūt, pl.: Tawāghīt	Designation of buildings that were worshiped as deities of deities in pre-Islamic Arabia, 2. In political Islam also as designation of the evil, corrupt system, 3. In Islamic theology designation of idolatry, i.e. the worship of another as Allah; thus, designation of persons who are not only unbelievers, but also want to persuade others against the will of Allah of the "rebellion against Allah"
Takfīr	the practice in Islamic jurisprudence and theology to accuse a Muslim or a group of Muslims of apostasy and thus declare them infidels (kuffar)
Tawfīq	(god given) success
Tawhīd	faith in the unity of god, confession of the unity of god, monotheism
Quraysh	Muhammad's Arab
Ummah	a religiously based community of Muslims that transcends tribal or clan boundaries as well as national borders
Wilāya, pl.: Wilāyāt	administrative district (in the Arabic cultural area)

"I will not forget here to praise the knights of [...], media, and other soldiers of the Khilafah and ask Allah to bless their jihad [...].

Their battle today is no less of importance than the military battle."[1]

(Rumiyah – issue 4)

---

[1] N.N. (2016d), online: <https://jihadology.net/category/rome-magazine/>, p. 7

Dedication

This master thesis is dedicated to my fallen friends, these two heroes gave their lives in the global war against terrorism in the desert of Afghanistan.

1 Introduction

1.1 Introduction to the theme

"Europa will continue to face an Islamist terrorist threat for the foreseeable future."[2]

Germany 2016 - 12 killed and 74 partly serious injured innocent citizens attacked by Islamic terrorists in one year, at well-known places and cities. 2016 was the year global Islamic terrorism reached Germany. Those terrorist acts have painfully pointed out that the threat posed by violent jihadists constitutes a high risk for national security – all over Europe and worldwide. Neumann sees Europe facing a "new wave of terrorism", with a new generation of jihadists, whose number has increased enormously in the past few years, consisting from mainly (very) young recruits.[3] In the age of globalization and social media they can publish their ideology in the shortest possible time all around the world in just a few seconds. This "new wave" is also characterized by a competition within the jihadist movement, which encourages attacks in the West.[4] These "new jihadists" cannot be seen as an isolated problem, they are inseparable associated with the events of the Arab Spring and the conflict in Syria and Iraq. These are the regions, where the Islamic State (IS)[5], with the proclamation of its caliphate, has claimed the leadership of the international and transnational operating armed Jihadist community for itself.[6] The IS has become the center point for the worldwide Jihadists' movement. Neumann tries to explain this development with the keywords – Utopia, inspiration and logistical hub.[7] Actually, the international community has no answer to this IS state-building project.[8]

---

[2] Rabasa & Benard (2015), p. 192

[3] cf. Neumann (2015), p. 13

[4] *ibid.*, p. 11

[5] There are many different names for the so called Islamic State (IS) – e.g. ISIS – *Islamic State of Iraq and Syria*, ISIL – *Islamic State of Iraq and the Levante* or DAESH – (acronym of Arabic name) *ad-daula al islāmiyya fī l-'Irāq wa-š-Šām*. In this scientific work, I will use IS in order to simplify the reading flow. I waive the addition "so called", without wanting to give the IS legitimacy.

[6] cf. Buchta (2015)

[7] cf. Neumann, *supra* note 4, p. 13

[8] cf. *ibid.*, p. 191

As a matter of fact, no other jihadist organization grown up as fast as IS in such a short period of time.[9,10]

Following the call of the self-proclaimed Caliph al-Baghdadi in 2014[11], round about 20.000 foreign fighters moved into the Iraq-Syria crisis area.[12] At least there are round about 4.000 Western Europeans among them[13] – thereunder approximately 800 Germans. According to current estimates, today around 2.000 "violent Islamists" are living in Germany.[14] Further, since 2015, there has been an increase in so-called "lone wolf's"[15] attacks all across Europe, too, which correlates with IS area losses in the Middle East.[16]

These figures show that the IS also offers a huge potential of attraction and radicalization for Western socialized people. The danger arising from radicalized, violent jihadists within Europe and other Western states should not to be underestimated – no matter whether they act as single persons or as members of large structures. The IS supports comparatively simple but extremely shocking terrorist attacks through its propaganda massively.[17] Like no other jihadist organization, it also stylizes individuals to heroes, who carry out small attacks against the "West-

---

9   cf. Roy (2015), online:
    <https://www.bka.de/SharedDocs/Downloads/EN/Publications/AutumnC onfer-
    ences/2015/herbsttagung2015RoyAbstract.html>

10 cf. Hughes & Vidino (2015), online: <https://cchs.gwu.edu/panel-discussion-isis-america-
    retweet s-raqqa>

11 Abu Bakr al-Bagdadi was born on July 28th in 1971 / Iraq. He claimed to be the next right-
    eous caliph and he announced the establishment of a worldwide caliphate on June 29th in
    2014 – the hour of birth of the Islamic State. According to the Russian government al-
    Bagdadi had been killed during an airstrike in Mai 2017.

12 cf. Spencer & Connor (2015), online:
    <http://www.telegraph.co.uk/news/worldnews/islamic-state /12038402/Number-of-
    foreign-fighters-in-Iraq-and-Syria-has-doubled-in-past-year.html>

13 cf. Neumann, *supra* note 3, p. 13

14 cf. Zeit online (2014), online: <http://www.zeit.de/politik/2014-06/Polizeigewerkschaft-
    Islamiste n>

15 Def.: "A terrorist or other criminal who acts alone rather than as part of a larger organiza-
    tion.";
  cf. Simpson & Weiner (2017), online: <https://en.oxforddictionaries.com/definition/lone_wolf>

16 cf. N.N. (2017), online: <http://www.spiegel.de/politik/ausland/terrorismus-in-europa-
    eine-chron ologie-a-1150645.html>

17 cf. Maaßen (2014), online:
    <https://www.verfassungsschutz.de/de/oeffentlichkeitsarbeit/publikati onen/pb-
    islamismus/faltblatt-2014-07-themenschwerpunkte-jihadistischer-propaganda>

ern crusaders" – as idols for every jihadist fighter.[18] It is noticeable, that there is not only an immediate threat of terror from the outside, but rather increasingly from the inside as well. For young Western jihadists, violence against the societies in which they grew up has become a legitimate means.

To describe the scope of this extraordinary challenge for the German security authorities following figures can be used: The phenomenon of officially called politically motivated foreign crime (PMAK), has grown considerably in Germany throw the last ten years. According to the statistics, PMAK cases increased from 902 (2007) to 2.719 (2017). If the development during the last years of the frequency number[19] of the general police criminal statistics is compared with the frequency number of the PMAK, following result can be determined: the general frequency number remained at a constant level – on the other hand – the frequency number of PMAK raised between 2007 and 2017 about 229%.[20] According to the report of the Federal Office for the Protection of the Constitution 2017, currently 24.400 Islamists are living in Germany,[21] thereof e.g. 4.070 in Bavaria – whereby 134 were classified "ready to use violence".[22] The "new wave of terrorism" requires that well-known measures and methods of security policy are reviewed. Neumann announced already 2015:

> "A new, comprehensive approach is needed – besides the traditional instruments of external and internal security, this is a strategic and credible approach in the fields of prevention, intervention and deradicalization."[23]

The challenges for security authorities in Western states are, in my opinion:

- understand how radicalization through the IS works,
- how to improve the prevention measures in this context and
- how to stop (and if necessary) respectively reverse the radicalization.

---

[18] cf. Neumann, *supra* note 3, p. 159

[19] extrapolation to 100 000 inhabitants

[20] view appendix 11.3. – evaluation political motivated crime Germany

[21] cf. BfV (2017), online: <https://www.verfassungsschutz.de/de/oeffentlichkeitsarbeit/publikatione n/verfassungsschutzberichte>, p. 160

[22] cf. BayLV (2017), online: <http://www.verfassungsschutz.bayern.de/ueberuns/medien/publikatio nen/index.html>, p. 295

[23] Neumann, *supra* note 4, p. 192

Therefore, a central component of the security policy of modern western states must be the fight against Islamic radicalization of parts of the population by international terrorist organizations like the IS. In this context, the role of the media for modern terrorist organizations should not be underestimated.[24]

One of the well-known speech tube of the IS propaganda, used for radicalization, is the online magazine "*Rumiyah*". IS media wing Al-Hayat released it in September 2016 in several different languages, including English, French, German, Russian, Indonesian and Uyghur. "*Rumiyah*" is Arabic for Rome, a reference to the fall of the Roman Empire – it replaces the first published online magazine "*Dabiq*".[25]

1.2 Question of research

In order to develop a corresponding counterstrategy, it is essential to recognize, which contents are used by IS propaganda and what kind of radicalization potential do they have. This leads me to the following question of research for my master thesis:

What are the contents of English-language propaganda published from the Islamic State in the online magazine "Rumiyah", which offer a radicalization potential for Western recipients?

The study opens by explaining the used category system and the way how it was built up. In this context the scientific findings (theoretical framework) about radicalization processes will be briefly summed up. Further the research material is introduced before the results of the analysis work will be discussed. Then the results will be compared to findings from secondary literature about the "*Dabiq*" magazine. At the end of the master thesis possible counter measures are discussed and pictured how they can be put into the practice exemplified on the deradicalization center of the Bavarian police. The thesis will close by reiterating the findings of the research and the limitations of those findings, and by identifying further areas of research on the topic.

In the appendix a bunch of definitions, facts about IS (history; political, social, historical and psychological logic of IS; IS's ideological and theological inclinations;

---

24 cf. Nitsch (2001), p. 293
25 cf. Mc Kernan (2016), online: <http://www.independent.co.uk/news/world/middle-east/isis-propa ganda-terror-group-losses-syria-iraq-a7228286.html>

IS in number and statistics) are listed. These facts are followed by a short analysis of the development of Islamic motivated crime in Germany. At the end of the appendix, the analyses datasheets have been added.

1.3 Limitations

Radicalization processes are individual and different research approaches are existing. This master thesis includes not all the leading theories extensively, only the essential parts are described (which were necessary for the creation of the used category system). For a detailed overview of the leading radicalization theories, please refer to Christmann[26] or Young et al.[27]. Additionally, next to the *"Rumiyah"* magazine a lot of other radicalization-books, -magazines, -websites etc. used by the IS are available. The findings referred to in point 4 are compared with an analogous study of the *"Dabiqe"* magazine by Kiefer et al.[28] in point 5. This master thesis not includes an examination or analyzation of the distribution channels for radicalization materials used by IS.

1.4 Method of research

In the core of my master thesis, methodically I oriented my analysis towards the qualitative content analysis according to Mayring.[29] During the analysis, I defined coding and context units, which consist of at least one subset (coding unit) – maximally several sentences (context unit). It must be noted, that a context unit is always a sense unit. So, sentences can have only one statement (meaning)[30]. These units will be analyzed by using a category system. Subsequently, the results were graphically processed, evaluated and discussed. The analysis work was carried out manually without the aid of an evaluation software.

Now the steps of the analysis will be explained briefly: Initially I derived deductively a category system from the scientific findings of the research on radicaliza-

---

[26] cf. Christmann (2012), online: <https://pure.hud.ac.uk/en/publications/preventing-religious-radic alisation-and-violent-extremism-a-syste>

[27] cf. Young, Zwenk & Rooze (2013), online: <http://www.terra-net.eu/files/publications/20140227 160036Literature%20review%20incl%20cover%20in%20color.pdf>

[28] cf. Kiefer et al. (2017), online: <http://journals.sfu.ca/jd/index.php/jd/article/view/75>

[29] Mayring (2010)

[30] cf. *ibid.*, p. 61

tion (focused on identified Jihadists' motifs - especially those that attract young people). Furthermore, where necessary, I created an inductive formation of sub-categories. Than the thirteen English written issues of the *"Rumiyah"* magazine (from September 2016 till September 2017) were evaluated using this category – system (in point 2 the built up of the category system itself is explained – the complete results of the analyses in detail are added in the appendix, point 11.4.). By carrying out a frequency analysis, the key focusses can be shown and after-wards interpreted. The method bases on an evaluation procedure that has already been applied at the Institute of Political Science at the Eberhard Karls University in Tübingen to evaluate the IS online magazine *"Dabiq"*[31]. Additionally, I de-scribed, how the layout of the different issues changed by the time based on this method (lightly modified, point 4.2.1.).

The theoretical framework part and the content about possible counter measures are based on literature work. The contents have been compiled from existing scholarly publications, the internet and scientific articles. The facts and scientific knowledge were collected and discussed subsequently.

1.5 Status and gap of research

A study of the radicalization discourse of IS has utmost value. Not merely from an academic purpose, it is vital to decipher and understand the radicalization tools used by IS. The narratives of IS need not only be comprehended, but also coun-tered and replaced with alternative narratives. In our world today, it is no longer enough to defeat these Islamic terrorists on a battlefield. Much more, their fanatic narratives must be fought online with a counter narrative. Consequently, to this end academics and experts across the world have been engaged with studying and analyzing the arise, structure and spread contents produced by IS. Particular-ly the *"Dabiq"* magazine was analyzed by many different scientists. Primarily aca-demics have been drawn towards focusing upon the process of radicalization trig-gered by propaganda material. There is a plethora of literature on the process of radicalization through propaganda material as well as on the IS's propaganda ef-forts, ranging from major publication like: Weiss & Hassan[32], Hall[33], Stern & Ber-

---

[31]   cf. Kiefer et al., *supra* note 29
[32]   Weiss & Hassan (2015)
[33]   Hall (2015)

ger [34] and Lahoud et al.[35] – to numerous shorter analytical texts, including those by Farwell[36], Friis[37], Peresin & Cervone[38], Böckler & Zick[39], Qadir[40], Colas[41] and Ingram & Reed[42].

Within their research, Weiss and Hassan, present the rise and expansion of the IS. Dozens of interviews with experts from the US military, various intelligence agents and former IS fighters focused intensely on how an almost defeated insurgent group could become a serious army of fanatical jihadists.

Hall first handed information by conducting narrative interviews directly with IS militants in Syria. In doing so, he not only presents the personal curricula vitae of individual fighters, but also explains why the Levant region will suffer for a long time from the long-term effects of IS's occupation.

In their work, Stern and Berger analyzed the new model of violent extremism that IS wants to incorporate into its own proclaimed caliphate in Iraq and Syria and implement it around the world. The analytical work traces the ideological innovations of the IS as well as the path of recruitment processes. The use of shocking pictures in this context is also discussed.

The report of Lahoud et al. identifies key areas where IS has demonstrated strength, learning and adaptive capacity. In contrast, weaknesses, flaws, and deficiencies in the field of ideology are also identified. To this end, the history of IS is drawn and compared with other prominent militant organizations (Al Qaeda and Taliban).

Farwell's work focuses on how IS uses brutal violence to establish its legitimacy. Here, the use of social media and cyber technology as a means of transport is discussed.

---

[34] Stern & Berger (2015)
[35] Lahoud et al. (2014)
[36] Farwell (2014)
[37] Friis (2015)
[38] Peresin & Cervone (2015)
[39] Böckler & Zick (2015)
[40] Qadir (2016)
[41] Colas (2016)
[42] Ingram & Reed (2017), online: <https://icct.nl/wp-content/uploads/2017/06/reeda_ingramh_instr uctionalmaterial.pdf>

The effect of IS produced splatter videos (showing beheadings) on the population in the United Kingdom and in the United States examined Friis. She illustrates the impact of the power of these images on American and British security discourse, too.

In their research Peresin and Cervone examined the role of women in the state construct of IS; distinguishes between the non-combat roles and the militant roles of women in this context. It also draws a situation picture of women who want to leave Europe (whose aim is to live in IS) and what problems can arise with female returnees.

Which specific motives for young Muslims in Germany are the reason why they are attracted to jihadism was examined by Böckler and Zick. Excessive demands in everyday life, the offered sense of community and the explanation of the world with simple truths are determined as the main factors here.

In that regard, particularly noteworthy are the anonymous case studies of Qadir. He demonstrates the numerous push-and-pull factors act on young people and detail the practical methods and solutions involved with changing permanently attitudes and behaviors.

Colas analyzed the "Dabiq" magazine in terms of targeted audiences and fundamentalist content. He explains the hermeneutics of IS in its media efforts to fathom the logic behind the messages.

Ingram and Reed explored the role of instructional material of the *"Inspire"* and *"Rumiyah"* magazine. In their work, the communication content of this propaganda magazines was analyzed and examined in more detail. As a result, strategic communication recommendations are proposed for possible proactively undermining extremist messaging as well as post-incident responding.

Because IS's global threat, research into all scientific disciplines in this context is being driven by the whole Western world. In my opinion, leaders in this field are the King's College London's "International Center for the Study of Radicalization and Political Violence", the West Point Military Academy's "Counter Terrorism Center" and the University of Leiden's "Terrorism and Political Violence Research Program". Regardless of these well credited academic ventures, there's still a gap in literature. Upon reviewing literature, an extreme dearth of available academic paperwork about the *"Rumiyah"* magazine, IS latest publication, can be seen. All the texts mentioned focus upon either *"Dabiq"* or other publications by terrorist organizations such as *"Inspire"* magazine by Al-Quaeda. The absence of literature on *"Rumiyah"* is troubling and demanding, however comprehensible – given to the timeline of *"Rumiyah's"* publication, they have been recently published and in fact are still being published. Apart from the scarcity of literature on *"Rumiyah"*, all the above-mentioned texts point towards the professional production graphic violence and proficient utilization of social media to account for the appeal and success of the IS productions. This research study deviates from these trends in the current literature at two fronts: first by focusing upon the magazine *"Rumiyah"* and second by focusing upon the triggers which succeeds to alter the recipient's perception and can start the radicalization process (radicalizes them to fight for IS's goals). By the rounding off comparison to the study of Kiefer et al. (point 5.), in which with a comparable category system the *"Dabiq"* magazine was evaluated, similarities of these two online magazines can be shown, but also their differences. The aim should be to present any identifiable changes in the radicalization triggers used by IS in its publications (which may be related to the substantial changes in IS territory). These results should help research and practice on prevention, intervention and deradicalization, and should allow governmental agencies to effectively tailor their strategies to the specific triggers of IS radicalization attempts.

2 Category System

2.1 Scientific findings of radicalization research (theoretical framework)

There is no final agreement on the exact definition of radicalization in scientific discourse. The understanding of radicalization as a process is a common ground –

"a personal and political transformation from one condition to another".[43]

However, theories on radicalization vary, as Young at al. wrote, especially with regard to their focus on different stages in this process, the importance they attach to socio-psychological factors, and whether an explanation of the process or a fight against it, is the goal of the research.[44] I understand radicalization not as an event, but as a process during which people's attitudes and thinking change.[45] Radicalization is an individual process that individuals go through in several phases, culminating in a form of extremism - often violent.[46,47] Furthermore, I see the key to the radicalization process in the phase of cognitive opening in which the individual becomes receptive to radical thoughts. It can be understood as the consequence of an individual crisis that can no longer be adequately processed and resolved by the hitherto accepted view of the world.[48] Such crises can be triggered by environmental (job loss, indebtedness, etc.), socio-cultural (such as racism or feeling of cultural inferiority), political (repression) or personal (death of a caregiver) negative experience.[49]

A special type of cognitive opening can also exist in people who suffer from mental illness. In some EU countries, especially in the Netherlands and the United Kingdom, the authorities have documented an extraordinary number of such cases in the context of radicalization.[50] Within the British *"Channel"* prevention program was discovered, that in 44% of 500 reported cases of radicalization, the rad-

---

[43] Christmann, *supra* note 27
[44] cf. Young, Zwenk & Rooze, *supra* note 28
[45] cf. Neumann (2013), p. 3
[46] cf. *ibid.*, p. 3
[47] cf. Young, Zwenk & Rooze, *supra* note 28
[48] cf. Wiktorowicz (2005), p. 20
[49] cf. *ibid.*, p. 20
[50] cf. Ritzmann (2017), p. 6

icalized persons are suspected or diagnosed with depression, anxiety disorders or other mental illnesses.[51] A Dutch health office reported that 60% of 300 *"jihadist radicals"* suffered from mental disorders, including 25% of serious mental illnesses.[52] The case numbers mentioned are notable but too small to be statistically or empirically relevant. In addition, studies of biographies of extremists in most European member states, including Germany, show no comparable results. But more research is obviously needed at this point. In my opinion, for the general susceptibility to extremist propaganda, the criterion "mental illness" cannot be decisive, because more than 99% of the affected group are not radicalizing.[53]

Nonetheless, regardless of the background of the mental opening, after it happened, radical ideologies can derive a new, meaningful interpretation of the world and those crises, escorted with simple and clear messages.[54] These ideologies often rely on simplified explanatory contexts, open up the recipient options for action and the prospect of recognition and security within a perceived as special community.[55] The term "ideology" is a controversial concept in science. In my thesis I focused on the approach of Snow:

> "[...] ideology is generally invoked as a cover term for the values, beliefs, and goals associated with a movement or a broader, encompassing social entity, and is assumed to provide the rationale for individual and collective action."[56]

As some concepts of radicalization suggest, ideologies and especially the social component of a shared world view do not only play a role in the beginning of a process of radicalization, they accompany the process at later stages, too.[57] For example, it is likely that the confirmation of one's perceived reality and ideology by the group, will result in an increasing tendency to extremism of the group

---

[51]   cf. Dodd (2016), online: <https://www.theguardian.com/uk-news/2016/may/20/police-study-radi calisation-mental-health-problems>

[52]   cf. Paulussen, Nijman & Lismont (2017), online: <https://icct.nl/wp-content/uploads/2017/03/IC CT-Paulussen-Nijman-Lismont-Mental-Health-and-the-Foreign-Fighter-Phenomenon-March-2017 -1.pdf>

[53]   About 25% of the German population suffers from diagnosed depression or anxiety disorders, so more than one million people receive inpatient treatment every year (https://de.statista.com/themen/1318/psychische-erkrankungen/).

[54]   cf. Roy, *supra* note 10

[55]   cf. Christmann, *supra* note 27

[56]   Snow & Scott (2007), p. 120

[57]   cf. Young, Zwenk & Rooze, *supra* note 28

members.[58] Radicalization research already recognizes specific motives for jihadist ideologies, which are considered to address and radicalize adolescents. Here, three major topics have been identified that potentially play a role in the radicalization of young people. These include deprivation experience by the adolescents (a vicarious victimization experience that feeds on a perceived worldwide deprivation of Muslims).[59] As an alternative and as a further central motif, Glaser names the promise to be part of a special connected society (like an elitist group or avant-garde). A third important motif is characterized by orientation and the creation of meaning by a demarcation from the majority society and a turn to another value system. [60]

Although the motif of deprivation is criticized by some authors[61] and is seen partly as a concomitant of other motives and not as an independent motif of radicalization[62], nonetheless I used it in my analysis. I believe that for recipients, especially for the second generation of Muslim migrants in the West, it has a role to play - not least because of their feeling of represented deprivation or their touched sense of justice.[63] This is above all a "perceived deprivation", a psychological phenomenon that leads the individual to feel himself and his fellow human beings (the same ethnic, religious, political or professional group) as disadvantaged and the whole society as unfair and closed. However, this may be the case even if society actually allows social mobility or the individual lives in relatively comfortable conditions.[64] Holman was able to confirm these motifs in his research on French Foreign Fighters[65], as well as Hegghammer, who dealt with Western jihadists in the Syrian conflict.[66] Saltman and Smith have also demonstrated the role of such

---

[58] cf. McCauley & Moskalenko (2008), p. 422

[59] cf. Glaser (2007), p. 5

[60] cf. *ibid.*, p. 6

[61] cf. Cesari & Pisoiu (2015), p. 10

[62] cf. Christmann, *supra* note 27

[63] cf. Briggs, Fieschi & Lownsbrough (2006), p. 45

[64] cf. Moghaddam (2005), p. 163

[65] cf. Holman (2015), online: <https://jamestown.org/program/the-swarm-terrorist-incidents-in-fran ce/>

[66] cf. Hegghammer (2013), online: <http://www.start.umd.edu/news/hegghammer-explains-variatio n-western-jihadists>

ideological jihadist motifs in their work on the radicalization and recruitment of Western women by IS.[67]

Among the communication partners of the radicalization process, besides the recipient, is the sender (in this case IS) - which offers the recipient new ideas and consciously or subconsciously picks up one or more of the above written motives. Propaganda is the central medium of their communication. Propaganda has an impact if and only if the individual context makes consumers receptive to it, especially in the phase of cognitive opening. In this context, I understand propaganda according to Bussmer as the communication of social groups that communicate their interests and values.[68] It moves within the "pluralistic propaganda paradigm" (which has emerged against the background of Western liberal democracies) – orienting itself on the psychological and social context of the target group.[69] The aim of propaganda, according to this paradigm, is to make an offer for the formation of identity, thereby enabling the recipient to be self-identified by offering guidance, interpretation, and behavioral instructions.[70] Since propaganda influences the radicalization process very individually, it is crucial for the effect of the content on the recipient how exactly the propaganda is tailored to his context. As a matter of fact, males and females from western countries are interested in the contents of IS – this suggests, that the offer of IS propaganda seems to contain potential radicalizing motives.[71,72]

As mentioned several times above, I believe that the phase of cognitive opening plays a special role - but I also recognize that propaganda is likely to influence the recipient at a later stage of radicalization. This means that propaganda not only recruits sympathizers (for example by confirmation), it consolidates and continues additional the radicalization process later. However, the results of this work cannot say anything about whether and what effect individual propaganda motifs have at which point in the radicalization process of individuals (these would be

---

[67]   cf. Saltman & Smith (2015), online: <https://www.isdglobal.org/wp-content/uploads/2016/02/Till_Martyrdom_Do_Us_Part_Gender_and_the_ISIS_Phenomenon.pdf>

[68]   cf. Bussemer (2005), p. 33

[69]   cf. *ibid.*, p. 53

[70]   cf. *ibid.*, p. 62

[71]   cf. Hughes & Vidino, *supra* note 11

[72]   cf. Prucha (2015)

objectives of psychological researches on recipients). Rather, the results present-ed here show which motifs are taken up by the transmitter in its communication, which can potentially have a radicalizing effect. In this thesis, I associate social-psychological radicalization research with a propaganda analysis and examine whether and to what extent the already known motifs (identified by the radicali-zation research) are contained in the propaganda of IS and how they are struc-tured in content.

2.2 Design of the category system

As explained in the previous part of the theoretical framework, I have based on the results of radicalization research for establishing my category system. It is grouped into the three main categories *"Deprivation"*, *"Social Relations and Affilia-tion"*, and *"Orientation and Meaningfulness"*. During the analysis, I defined coding and context units, which consist of at least one subset (coding unit) – maximally several sentences (context unit). It must be noted, that a context unit is always a sense unit. So, sentences can have only one statement (meaning).[73] In passages in which statements are substantiated by longer tracts, I have encoded the state-ment only once. I have doubly coded and strictly divided the two categories of *"concept of the enemy"* and *"deprivation"* because of their proximity to content. Furthermore, it must be noted that it was difficult in some cases to divide the cat-egories *"concept of the enemy - wrong religion"* and *"delimitation to the majority"* (in context of the Muslim world outside the IS). By the way, each issue of *"Rumi-yah"* forms one analysis unit.

2.2.1 Deprivation

As the first main category, *"Deprivation"* is defined as expressing one's own per-ceived victimhood in western majority society and / or as a community of faith in the world. Coded were meaning units that describe the individual suppression of "true" Muslims in Western societies, the worldwide suppression of Islam, or at-tacks on IS as a representative of the *"Ummah"*. Likewise, sense units were encod-ed which represent the actions of IS as self-defense (due to deprivation). In con-trast to the other main categories, no subcategories were derived or inductively formed within the main category of *"Deprivation"*. Anchor example:

---

[73] cf. Mayring, *supra* note 30, p. 61

"They carried on with their pacifist and even pro-democracy da'wah while Muslim woman around the world were being abused, vilified, imprisoned, and violated at the hands of the kuffar and their puppets."[74]

2.2.2 Social Relations and Affiliation

This main category includes statements that describe group-specific characteristics of IS, which also include moral and material benefits, as well as those that emphasize community within IS. This main category includes the following categories:

"*Superiority of IS*": This category includes all representations and assertions of IS's own power and military strength. Often these representations are related to threats against the enemies of IS. However, these threats contain no direct calls for destruction. However, an enumeration of individual successes is encoded in the category "*Achievement of IS*". Anchor example:

"The Americans faced a great massacre, to the extent that many of them were seen fleeing from the battle, hiding in Muslims' houses. At first, the mujahidin refrained from entering those homes for fear of harming the Muslims, but once they confirmed the presence of the American troops inside them, they found them hiding like cowards and began killing them as if they were beetles and flies, and all excellence and blessing belong to Allah."[75]

"*IS as Avant-garde*": All representations of the IS and its members are listed here as the chosen and the only legitimate representatives of god. Anchor example:

"As for the mujahidin in Allah's cause – and they are the elite of His creation, those of His slaves whom He has chosen to become martyrs and whom He subjects to favorable tests – then the death of their leaders and commanders who stormed ahead of them into battle, running head first into hardships for their religion, only increases their firmness and determination in fighting the enemies of Allah."[76]

"*Achievement of IS*": As IS achievements, I understand all the accounts of the group's achievements, including both military victories, successful assassinations, territorial expansion, and membership growth (*"bay'ah"*). Anchor example:

---

[74] N.N. (2016a), online: <https://jihadology.net/category/rome-magazine/>, p. 15

[75] N.N. (2017a), online: <https://jihadology.net/category/rome-magazine/>, p. 9

[76] N.N., *supra* note 75

> "Meanwhile, the soldiers of the Islamic State succeeded in damaging 4 Abrams tanks, destroying 16 hummers, [...] Additionally, several members of the Rafidi army and their militias were killed and wounded."[77]

"Social Security": This category summarizes those statements that refer to social and material security within IS – with social security as the emphasis on equality in their so-called state. To delineate this category of *"IS as Avant-garde"*, I have encoded only statements about current, not future, conditions. Anchor example:

> "[...] the amir of the Central Office for Investigating Grievances clarified the reason behind the office's establishment, and the role it plays in eliminating the injustices that might afflict both the subjects and soldiers of the Islamic State. [...]"[78]

2.2.3 Orientation and Meaningfulness

This main category is defined as expressions which on the one hand point to the need for a meaningful, clear world view with higher goals, and at the same time point out possibilities and rules of action. This main category includes the following categories and subcategories:

"Clear rules": This code unit includes concrete behavioral instructions that cover the entire life, from everyday life to jihad. In addition to the direct specification of rules, descriptions of punishments due to misconduct were also coded. Anchor example:

> "This form of jihad (the jihad through du'a) is more emphasized in the case of those for whom Allah exempted from fighting for His cause, such as woman, the ill, the disabled, and the imprisoned. They should all make du'a for the mujahidin, for indeed, when Allah excused the exempted, [...]"[79]

"Concept of the enemy": Content of the category is the clear juxtaposition, respectively dividing the world into e.g. good and evil or believing and disbelieving. While there is sometimes a direct comparison to the positive IS, I also have encoded one-sided naming of enemies. These are explicitly pejorative statements. During the analysis, I inductively formed three subcategories in this category to

---

[77] *ibid.*, p. 25
[78] *ibid.*, p. 10
[79] N.N. (2016c), online: <https://jihadology.net/category/rome-magazine/>, p. 33

differentiate the various enemy concepts. Decisive for an assignment was the subject of IS speaks and not the reason for the denigration:

- *"Wrong religion"*: This subcategory contents statements concerning those individuals and groups (and their behaviors) attached to the false religion, even the "false" Islam. That means, the individuals and groups are characterized not by their affiliation to the West or any other jihadist group, but by their affiliation to a false religion. Also, the general dichotomy of the world in infidels. Anchor example:

  "An individual is not saved form the filth and impurity of shirk and its people as long as he does not disbelieve in the tawaghit of his era, [...] Also included is the "Murtadd Brotherhood" group and its parties, factions and sister organizations, [...]"[80]

- *"the West and Allies"*: This subcategory includes negative statements about Western nation states, including Russia, Saudi Arabia, and Japan, as well as all entities that cooperate with them, such as Israel or "the Jews," Arab states and rebel groups in the Syrian civil war (IS's point of view). In addition, the Assad regime, as well as Muslim scholars supporting the West, have been included in this subcategory. Finally, I also coded Western concepts such as nationalism or secularism into this subcategory. Anchor example:

  "The old colonialism was but a front for the Crusaders, just as it is today a front for the Jews and Christians. Indeed, the "Caesar of Rome" Bush has declared multiple times that, "It is a Crusade!""[81]

- *"other jihadist groups"*: Here the demarcation to other jihadist groups was encoded, which did not submit themselves to the IS. These include, for example, Al-Qaeda and the Al-Nusra Front (now: Jabhat Fatah Al-Sham). Anchor example:

  "Fighting the Islamic State ultimately became a joint project between the Taliban movement and the nations of kufr, who were terrified by the presence of the Islamic

---

80 N.N., *supra* note 75
81 N.N. (2016b), online: <https://jihadology.net/category/rome-magazine/>, p. 19

State on their borders, just as its presence terrified the United States of America, which occupies Afghanistan."[82]

"Supposed noble targets": Statements of this category express the supposedly higher and long-term goals of the Islamic State, excluding direct appeals to annihilate the enemy. Anchor example:

"We ask Allah to strengthen the mujahidin of the Islamic State, so they may liberate Makkah and Madinah from the tawaghit of Al Salul - may Allah disgrace them - and to bless us with hajj and 'umrah in the shade of the Shari'ah."[83]

"Adventure and borderline experience": In this category should be encoded the advertisement for involvement in the IS's struggle, which is presented as an individual adventure and challenge. This should be done by exemplifying the allegedly exciting and adventurous experiences of IS fighters. This category has been included in the analysis for comparability with the analysis work about the *"Dabiq"* magazine from the secondary literature. In my analysis, no sense units could be identified that would have been subsumed under this purely (if then this category was marginalized, but the main context was different).

"Delimitation to the majority": In this category, those units of meaning were encoded, which describe the majority society in the West or even the majority Muslims and contrast them with the otherness and strangeness of the "true" Muslims. This also includes direct calls to differentiate the behavior and norms of the majority society or the majority Muslims as well as examples of persons who have successfully distinguished themselves. Anchor example:

"Thus, a person cannot be a Muslim except by adhering to Islam in both of these aspects, so whoever doesn't submit to Allah – such as one who abandons all actions or forcefully resists some of the manifest, mutawatir rulings – is nothing but a kafir, and whoever isn't exclusively for Allah – such as one who worships the prophets and the righteous, whether blindly following others or having misunderstandings – is nothing but a mushrik, even if he prays, fasts, and claims that he is a Muslim."[84]

"Call for change and action": This refers to the direct and indirect call to action, such as emigration to the caliphate and the call to jihad or the annihilation of the

---

[82]   N.N., *supra* note 76
[83]   N.N., *supra* note 75
[84]   *ibid.*, p. 5

opponents as well as the call for terrorist acts in Western countries. As direct calls, I have coded second-person singular or plural phrases and indirect calls (sentence constructions with auxiliary verbs such as "should"). Anchor example:

> "Kill them on the streets of Brunswick, Broadmeadows, Bankstown, and Bondi. Kill them at the MCG, the SCG, the Opera House, and even in their backyards. Stab them, shoot them, poison them, and run them down with your vehicles."[85]

2.2.4 Uncoded sense units

All sense units that could not be clearly identified and classified with these radicalization triggers have been grouped in this category. This does not mean that their content cannot also promote radicalization – these areas could not be subsumed under the category system mentioned. The quantitative representation of these *"uncoded sense units"* was made to represent the ratio of all coded and uncoded areas.

2.3 Interim conclusion

To carry out the quantitative content analysis of the *"Rumiyah"* magazine, a category system was developed. This system was built on the current scientific knowledge of radicalization research. Thus, these scientific findings form the theoretical framework of the entire analysis work.

Basically, there is no final agreement on the exact definition of radicalization in scientific discourse. Common ground is the understanding of radicalization as a process. All the theories about radicalization vary, especially regarding their focus on different stages in this process, the importance they attach to socio-psychological factors and whether the author aims an explanation of the process or a fight against it. The key to the radicalization process is the phase of cognitive opening – at this time-slot the recipient becomes susceptible to radical thoughts. The cognitive opening is usually the consequence of an individual crisis triggered by environmental, socio-cultural, political, or personal negative experience. The special case of cognitive opening caused by mental illnesses is negligible. Once the cognitive opening is done, radical ideologies can derive a new, meaningful interpretation of the world and crises, escorted with simple and clear messages. Three major motifs for jihadist radicalization have been identified in research literature

---

[85] *ibid.*, p. 17f

- the promise to be part of a special connected society (like an elitist group or avant-garde); a vicarious victimization experience that feeds on a perceived worldwide deprivation of Muslims (deprivation); orientation and the creation of meaning by a demarcation from the majority society and a turn to another value system (orientation and meaningfulness).

Because of the awareness that only the individual context makes the consumer receptive to Islamism contents, IS uses to western recipients tailored propaganda in its communication. Due to the fact that among the followers of these propaganda media is a not to be despised number of men and women of the Western world, the offer of IS propaganda seems to contain potential radicalizing motives. To identify the frequency of critical factors that can trigger or promote radicalization, the content of the *"Rumyiah"* magazine has been analyzed using the following category system:

The three main categories are "deprivation", "orientation and meaningfulness", "social relationship and affiliation".

Firstly, the category *"deprivation"* is not divided in further subcategories. Secondly, the main category *"social relationship and affiliation"* is split up into categories: *"superiority of IS"*, *"IS as avant-garde"*, *"Achievements of IS"* and *"social security"*. Thirdly, the main category *"orientation and meaningfulness"* is divided in the categories *"concept of the enemy"*, *"clear rules"*, *"supposed noble targets"*, *"adventure and borderline experience"*, *"delimitation to the majority"* and *"call for change"*. In the category *"concept of the enemy"* the subcategories *"wrong religion"*, *"the west and allies"* and *"other jihadist groups"* are pictured.

All sense units that could not be clearly identified and classified with these categories have been summed up in *"uncoded sense units"*.

In context of the analysis, each issue of *"Rumiyah"* forms one analysis unit.

3 Description research material

3.1 Islamic State and new media

IS is commonly considered one of the greatest threats of our time. With its murderous ideology and its attacks all over the Western world, but especially on local targets in its sphere of influence, it represents a global challenge for security agencies, governments, civil society actors and further stakeholders. IS follows and reinforces the observable trend that extremist actors are increasingly active on the Internet. Europol already noted in 2012 that the Internet is now the primary communication medium for extremist groups and individuals.[86] IS has perfected the use of this medium and is considered to be the most successful actor among the extremist groups in this field so far.[87]

Using mass media by jihadist groups to spread their point of view is not a new phenomenon. Zelin[88] has shown in his study four phases of the dissemination of jihadi media. Beginning in the mid-1980s with analogue published essays, magazines and videotapes, the trend with the development of the Internet towards jihadist websites changed during the 1990s. At the beginning of the 2000s, a change to interactive forums took place in which like-minded people could exchange their ideas. With the advent and proliferation of social media such as Facebook or Twitter, publications have increasingly shifted to these platforms.[89] 2002 Osama bin Landen wrote a letter to one of his Taliban leaders, that shows, the use of mass media for earlier groups was already meaningful:

> "It is obvious that media war in this century is one of the strongest methods; in fact, its ratio may reach 90% of the total preparation for the battles."[90]

Now the door was open – henceforth internet is being used for various purposes (previously unknown opportunities and as real important fact, outsiders have difficulty accessing the closed groups). These include, but are not limited to, fund-

---

86 cf. Wainwright (2017), p. 6

87 cf. Winter (2014), online: <http://icsr.info/2017/02/icsr-report-media-jihad-islamic-states-doctrin e-information-warfare/>, p. 6f

88 cf. Zelin (2015)

89 cf. *ibid.*, p. 88f

90 Bin Laden (2002), online: <https://ctc.usma.edu/harmony-program/letter-to-mullah-muhammed-umar-from-bin-laden-original-language-2/>, p. 2

raising, targeted planning and control of actions, propaganda, and opportunities for radicalization and mobilization.[91] (The way of planning such an assault can proceed is illustrated, for example, by Hughes and Meleagrou-Hitchens; they call such planning actors *"Virtual Entrepreneurs"*.[92]) The publication of content tailored to the intended user is actually another option the internet.[93] IS also uses this possibility by publishing content tailored to the Western audience. This content for the West is published by the Al-Hayat Media Center.[94]

3.2 Al Hayat Media Center – the media department

In the spring of 2014, IS began building up its own media house - the Al-Hayat Media Center[95] (*"Al-Hayat"* is the Arabic term for *"the life"*). There is no connection between the Al-Hayat Media Center and the London's Arabic newspaper with the same name, which is pan-Arab and Western-oriented. IS's media center publishes various own publications of media for prospective and future recruits. From the guide-book to the well-known videos of decapitations and combat missions. Normally the contents are offered for download not only in Arabic, but also in English, German and French.[96] The media activities of IS were previously managed centrally. However, with the death of the head of Al-Hayat Media Center in the late summer of 2016, it is assumed that controlling the media activities in the future could be much less centralized.[97] Currently, there is even a general decline in IS online activity. First, recently published studies point in this direction (exemplified stated by Lakomy in 2017[98]), although further comparable studies are needed.

---

[91] cf. Weimann (2015), pp. 24–36

[92] Hughes & Meleagrou-Hitchens (2017)

[93] cf. Weimann, *supra* note 92, pp. 24–36

[94] cf. Gambhir (2016), pp. 20–26

[95] view appendix point 11.2.5 – overview IS media departments

[96] cf. Schubert (2015), online: <https://www.pro-medienmagazin.de/gesellschaft/weltweit/2015/11/ 23/brutal-und-schnell-die-medienstrategie-des-is/>

[97] cf. Zelin (2018), online: <https://jihadology.net/category/al-%E1%B8%A5ayat-media-center/>

[98] Lakomy (2017)

3.3 "Rumiyah" – the magazine

One of the multidimensional communication strategy's most imperative component consist of IS publication in the form of an online magazines available readily
through the deep internet. IS periodically publishes lustrous propaganda magazines, with the primary aims of recruiting new members from the West and other
parts of the world, raise funds and spread their propaganda.[99] The issues of the
magazines are sophisticated, slick and aesthetically appealing. To add to this, they
are also printed in several languages, including English and German. Currently
there are two magazines available online from the IS – "Dabiq" (discontinued) and
"Rumiyah". The Clarion Project posts the issues of these magazines online with the
intentions of moving forward towards fulfilling the academic aspirations of understanding the ideologies of the IS.[100] "Dabiq" is the IS's first propaganda magazine. There are currently 15 issues of "Dabiq" available online after it was discontinued. The first issue of the magazine appeared in July 2014.[101] "Dabiq" proclaims itself to be a

> "[...] periodical magazine focusing on the issues of tawhid (unity), manhaj (truth-
> seeking), hijrah (migration), jihad (holy war) and jama'ah (community). It will also
> contain photo reports, current events and informative articles on matters relating to
> the Islamic State [...]"[102]

The magazine focuses and portrays IS as they imagine and picture themselves to
be. Its rhetoric and design avowals and further brags about the victories of the IS,
while simultaneously romanticizing about the reestablishment of an Islamic gold-
en age with the instalment of a new caliphate through a holy war.[103] The magazine's name is equally symbolic and telling as the rest of the publication's content.
Dabiq refers to the place in the northern countryside of Syria, which is prophe-

---

[99] cf. Ingram (2016), p. 459

[100] cf. N.N. (2014), online: <https://clarionproject.org/islamic-state-isis-isil-propaganda-
magazine-dabiq-50/>

[101] cf. ibid.

[102] ibid., p. 5

[103] cf. ibid.

sized in Islamic tradition to be the place where the apocalyptic war between the *"right"* and the *"wrong"* will take place near Armageddon.[104]

In September 2016, IS revamped their media and propaganda strategy. This was understandably due to the losses suffered by IS in the territories which they occupied. IS had earlier occupied the region of Dabiq, however in October 2016 they were driven out of the town of Dabiq by the Turkish military and Syrian rebels.[105]

IS's media and propaganda team was quick to respond and realign their strategic communication plan by ceasing the publications of *"Dabiq"* and initiating the publication of a new magazine with the name *"Rumiyah"*.

The change in name has prompted media speculation. Is the change from *"Dabiq"* to *"Rumiyah"* a sign that IS is under extreme pressure from unrelenting airstrikes or is it just a savvy public relation decision?[106] It has also been reported that *"Rumiyah"* lacks the fire and brimstone apocalyptic narrative of *"Dabiq"*, is shorter than its forerunner, and lacks the unifying theme of other IS propaganda tools.[107] Comerford suggested that the change in name of the magazine might signal a shift in emphasis from a physical caliphate to a more virtual one.[108] There are currently 13 issues of *"Rumiyah"* available online.

---

[104] cf. Ryan (2014), online: <https://jamestown.org/program/hot-issue-dabiq-what-islamic-states-ne w-magazine-tells-us-about-their-strategic-direction-recruitment-patterns-and-guerrilla-doctrine/>

[105] cf. Joscelyn (2016), online: <https://www.longwarjournal.org/archives/2016/10/town-of-dabiq-falls-to-turkish-backed-forces.php>

[106] cf. McKernan (2016), online: <https://www.independent.co.uk/news/world/middle-east/isis-propaganda-terror-group-losses-syria-iraq-a7228286.html>

[107] *ibid.*

[108] cf. Comerford (2016), online:
<https://www.newstatesman.com/politics/staggers/2016/10/what-isis-lost-dabiq>

Issue	Release Date	Pages
1	September 5th, 2016	38
2	October 4th, 2016	38
3	November 11th, 2016	46
4	December 7th, 2016	40
5	January 6th, 2017	44
6	February 4th, 2017	44
7	March 7th, 2017	38
8	April 4th, 2017	48
9	May 4th, 2017	58
10	June 17th, 2017	46
11	July 13th, 2017	60
12	August 6th, 2017	46
13	September 9th, 2017	44

Figure 1: Issues of the „Rumiyah" magazine - overview

The new magazine is shorter than the previous IS publication and can be seen as a continuation of it. *"Rumiyah"* aims at elucidating upon and prompting the political and theological ideologies of IS and further discouraging opposition to IS by reveling about terrorism operations conducted by them.[109]

The title *"Rumiyah"* refers to Rome which IS now desires to conquer. Keeping in line with the symbolism which is prevalent in IS produced content. Conquering Rome is not only a political victory, but also emblematic. IS interprets the Western Civilization as a continuation of the ancient Roman Empire. Hence, aiming to take over Rome is alike taking down the West in its entirety emblematically.[110]

3.4 Interim conclusion

The global fight against IS, one of the greatest threats of our time, is one of the hardest global challenges for security and governmental agencies since decades. The primary communication medium for Islamist terrorist organizations and their followers is the internet. Further, they realized already in the early 2000s that the future of their communication networks can only be secured in social

---

[109] cf. N.N., *supra* note 101
[110] cf. *ibid.*

media and other virtual closed groups. In those days they started their "fight on the virtual battlefield" with fundraising, targeted planning and control of actions, propaganda, and opportunities for radicalization and mobilization.

Actually, IS showed after a short period of time, that it mastered this way of acting perfectly. Al-Hayat Media Center, IS's official media Department, was and is publishing content tailored to the Western audience successfully (successfully means in this context, they had a big fast grown and still growing community of followers). They offer their products in different languages not only in Arabic, but also in English, German and French.

The flagship of IS's Al-Hayat Media Center is the *"Rumiyah"* magazine. It replaced the *"Dabiq"* magazine – its forerunner. *"Rumiyah"* is a high performed magazine available online. The issues are sophisticated, slick and aesthetically appealing. There are currently 13 issues available online. In this master thesis these issues of the *"Rumiyah"* magazine will be analyzed by a content analysis (point 4.). The results will be compared with the results of similar analyses from secondary literature of the *"Dabiq"* magazine (point 5.).

4 Results of the analysis

Overall, 13 issues of the "*Ruminyah*" magazine were analyzed. It was a total of 590 pages of research material that consisted of texts, images, and graphics. The results of the analysis work are presented below, first the analysis of the content, then the analysis of the layout. Detailed overviews and graphics of the analysis can be found in the appendix point 11.4.2.. A download of the individual issues of "*Rumiyah*" magazine (research material) as well as the evaluation forms for the individual issues were saved on the data medium enclosed with the master thesis.[111]

4.1 Content analysis

4.1.1 General findings

The content of the 590 pages was divided into 3.939 sense units. Since the number of pages of the editions and the number of pictures and graphics printed in the editions varied, so does the number of sense units per issue.

---

[111] There is a research material folder on the disk that stores all 13 issues of the "*Ruminyah*" magazine. In order not to commit an offence of disseminating violent media, this folder has been encrypted. The password can be requested via the author of this thesis.

Treemap - total results analysis of "*Ruminyah*" magazine (issue 1 - 13)

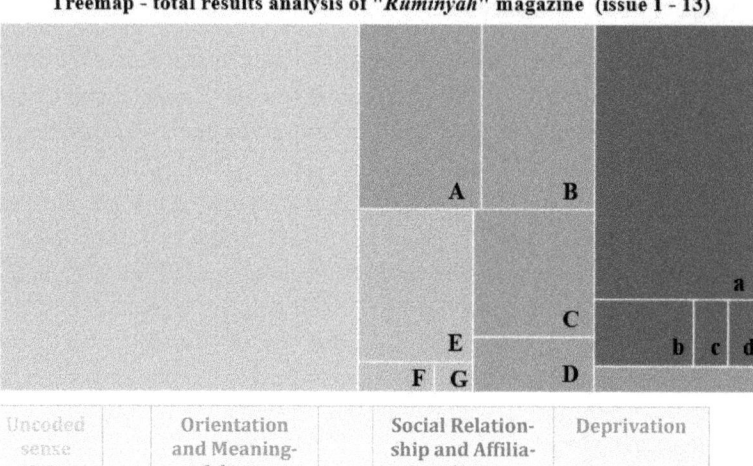

Uncoded sense Units		Orientation and Meaning- fulness		Social Relation- ship and Affilia- tion	Deprivation
	A	Delamination to the majority	a	Achievement of IS	
	B	Clear rules	b	IS as Avant-garde	
	C	Call for change and action	c	Superiority of IS	
	D	Supposed no- ble targets	d	Social Security	
		Concept of the enemy			
	E	Wrong religion			
	F	The West and Allies			
	G	Other Jihadist groups			

Figure 2: Treemap total results of the analysis work

It can be stated, that 40.92% of the sense units were uncoded ones. The 59.08% of the encoded area can be broken down as follows: 35.26% fall under the main category "*Orientation and Meaningfulness*", 21.96% under the main category "*Social Relationship and Affiliation*", and 1.85% under the main category "*Deprivation*". To illustrate the total result, the treemap shown above was prepared. The results in detail are presented and discussed in the following:

4.1.2 Deprivation

Of the total of 3.939 sense units, 1.85% was attributed to the main category "*Deprivation*", which represents only a small proportion among the main categories. The share moved within the issues between 0.9% and 2.1%. Individual discrepancies from averages existed in issue no. 7 with 5.3%, in issue No. 9 with 2.8%, and issue no. 12 with 3.0%. Issue no.7 dealt with the establishing of the IS. In the reports were therefore more arguments for the founding of the state in the field, which are attributable to the "*Deprivation*". Issue No. 9 is subtitled "*The ruling on the belligerent Christians*". In this context, a speech was printed made by Shaykh Abul-Hasan Al-Muhajir (one of the "official" spokesman of the IS). Issue No. 12 makes the fight for Raqqah a subject of discussion. In this context, more sense units were used that represent the "suffered" deprivation.

This category deals with the portrayal of the global victimhood of Sunni Muslims (the *Ummah*). In many cases, above all, the West is described as the enemy and oppressor of the *Ummah* and its faith. Muslims, especially women and children, are portrayed as innocent victims of structural and personal violence. In this context, every single Muslim represents with his victimhood the entire *Ummah*. Elsewhere, attacks on the IS are stylized as attacks on the entire *Ummah* – IS sees itself as a proxy for the *Ummah*, against which a conspiracy is assumed.

From the IS's point of view the Western media are evil, too, because they report wrongly about it and its fighters. Thus, they also contribute to the suppression of the IS. IS also addresses the suggested unequal treatment and oppression in Western countries. The construction of a victim role is crucial for offering a concept of the enemy and a regarded solution strategy. Only when the personal crisis is placed in a wider context of deprivation, the responsibility for the crisis can be attributed to external actors. IS then shows the recipient the way out of the crisis in the form of its clear rules and presentations of clear defined enemies.

In summary, however, it could be noted that the authors of the "*Rumiyah*" magazine obviously did not make "*Deprivation*" to a priority topic of their journal (due to its small share), nevertheless, from the point of view of radicalization research, it is an important part of content.

4.1.3 Social Relations and Affiliation

The main category "*Social Relationship and Affiliation*" made up a total of 21.96% of the encoded sense units (total number 865). This main category is divided into four categories whose frequency can be presented well by the following pie chart:

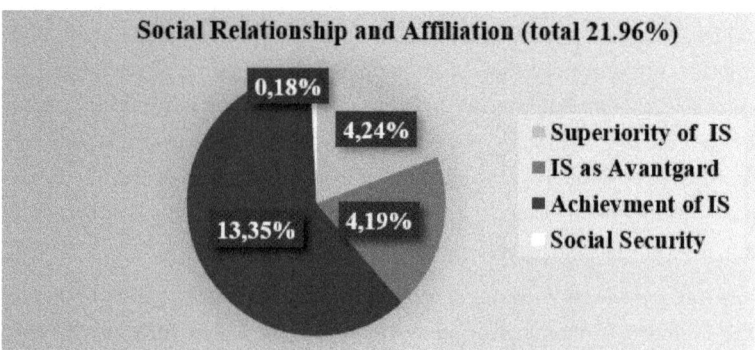

Figure 3: Pie chart partition – "Social Relationship and Affiliation"

The category "*Achievment of IS*" dominates within this main category with a total share of 13.35%. The reason therefor is that within every issue of "*Rumiyah*" magazine a report entitled "*Operations*" (later "*Military and Covered Operations*") is printed. In this series, the individual achievements of the IS in the war zones of the Middle East and individual outstanding terrorist attacks (world-wide committed) are presented. This share is an integral part of each issue. In several editions there are additional single pages with a more detailed description of victories in special battles. A significant accumulation in one of the issues could not be determined. When general coverage, interviews or speeches are brought to the fore, the proportion is somewhat lower.

By presenting its successes, the size and power of IS should be underlined and thus give it enough authority for future orientation and meaning. The IS presents its achievements in such a way that the uniqueness and thereby its legitimacy of the respective "project" is underlined. At the beginning, the authors directly refer to territorial expansions of the area of influence – later, more and more smaller successes are presented. Many accomplishments are attributed to the omnipotence of Allah, describing in particular the annihilation of enemies as their righteous punishment of Allah. Ultimately, this indirectly expresses the exclusive representation claim of the group (see also "*IS as Avant-garde*"). Attacks in the Western world are described as military successes, with the IS praising the successful fighters and underscoring its global claims. By naming its achievements, IS constructs an output legitimacy as genuine state or caliphate. Precisely for this reason, in all editions is consistently printed above mentioned series *"Operations"*, which is dedicated this category.

Content subsumed under the category *"Superiority of IS"* is continuously at the same level. Striking is a peak in issue no. 9 – in this issue the superiority of Islam to Christendom (Islam here as it is taught in the IS) is presented in detail. A similar situation is in the category *"IS as Avant-garde"*. The number of sense units rank at a constant level here, too – except for a peak in the second issue. Reason for this is the first part of the report *"The religion of Islam and the Jama'ah of the Muslims"* and the start of the series *"Paths to Victory"*.

These two categories consistently contain positive self-descriptions of the IS – once regarding the undeniable superiority of the IS and once regarding the presentation of the IS as a superior conspiratorial community. Many passages in this regard deal with the religious legitimacy of the caliphate and its members through Allah and his messenger. IS is described as a currently unique and historical phenomenon whose existence is due to the direct will of Allah. The self-description of the IS as a genuine caliphate expresses its universal claim to command all Sunni Muslims, too. Struggles, led by soldiers of other Muslim countries, against the IS are portrayed as hostility, which proves all the more that the IS is the "right caliphate". Again, and again, the right to exist of the IS is justified by giving the Muslims rights, dignity, power and leadership; only the IS could defend the "believers" from the "disbelievers".

Under category *"Social Security"* summable contents appeared only in the first four editions. The number of sense units to be counted in this context is small. The authors of *"Ruminyah"* magazine have evidently shifted their focus on conveying the feeling of *"Social Relationship and Affiliation"* by using the already mentioned three other categories.

4.1.4 Orientation and Meaningfulness

With a share of 35.26% within the whole sense units, the main category *"Orientation and Meaningfulness"* represents the largest part of the coded area (total number 1.389). Again, the percentage breakdown into the associated categories and subcategories can best be illustrated by a combined pie and bar chart:

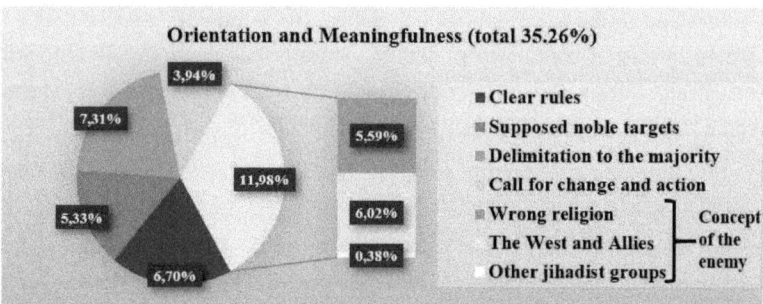

Figure 4: Combined chart partition – "Orientation and Meaningfulness"

"Concept of the enemy", with a total of 11.98%, accounted for the largest share within this main category. Within this category, the sub-category *"the West and Allies"* was the most represented with a share of 6.02%, followed closely by the sub-category *"wrong religion"* with a share of 5.59%. Rarely text passages could be assigned to the subcategory *"other jihadist groups"* (0.38%).

To the sub-category *"the West and Allies"* are counted the US and Europe, as well as Russia, Spain, Australia and especially Israel, as well as most Arab regimes, such as Saudi Arabia, and many rebel groups who are fighting in the Syrian civil war (which cooperate with the West in some way). Anyone who interacts with the West (*"the Crusaders"*, *"the servants of the cross"*) and does not side with the IS becomes an enemy that is negated, vilified or ridiculed. The dividing lines between the USA, Europe, Arab regimes, etc. are blurred in the presentation of the IS, since the addressees are often not separated from one another.

Particularly often, the West and its allies are called opponents of the Islamic world, who want to impose their rule on Muslims in a global crusade. Here, the West is described as arrogant and cruel, as manipulative and exclusively on its own advantage considered. Again, and again Nationalism, secularism and democracy as Western concepts appear, which are imposed on Muslims – they are presented strongly negatively, especially for the Islamic world where this way of life as not authentic (in the spirit of IS). But while IS attributes the role of the aggressor to the West, paradoxically, in other places, they are vilified as cowardly, weak and as bad fighters. The West and its allies are seen as indifferent and inhuman, too. At the same time, propaganda paints a picture of IS as the savior, the savior of humanity, especially for the *Ummah*, before the oppression and tyranny of these regimes.

To the subcategory "*other jihadist groups*" can be noted, that other jihadist groups were considered with only a few passages. However, the IS is adept at referring to prominent jihadist pioneers like Osama Bin Laden and put itself in this tradition and denying this place to other jihadist groups by declaring itself to the only applicably benchmark. Taken as a whole, this subcategory highlights IS's claim to leadership in the global jihad by using the negative portrayal of other jihadist groups. The "accumulation" of seven encoded sense units in issue no. 10 can be justified by the report "*The murtadd Taliban movement*", in which the authors talk extensively about the Taliban.

IS sees itself as the sole representative of the "true" Islam and thus of the will of Allah. This subcategory "*wrong religion*" takes second place within the "*concept of the enemy*" – with almost as many encoded sense contexts as "*the West and Allies*" (220 to 237). The "true" Muslims, as the IS designates his followers, are confronted to non-Muslims faiths, like Christians, Jews and atheists as well as followers of other faiths of Islam. In some cases, IS has distanced itself from "false" religious communities without justification. This happens specifically, for example, in the combined report series "*Establishing the Islamic State*" and "*The Twelver rafidah*" (Issue no. 7 – no. 11). By clear demarcations a friend / enemy Dichotomy should be produced. All those who do not follow the IS's interpretation of Islam are enemies, since only the IS represents the "true" Islam. Persistent the IS refers to the historical continuity of his concept of the enemy to underline his two-part world view. The representation of the "false" religious communities is often linked to a prophetic scenario in which the "false" religions will perish. Godliness often plays a role, but those who do not live godly, would be punished by Allah, while "true" Muslims would be rewarded as the heirs of the true faith. The subcategory "*wrong religion*" shows, that there is a metaphysical struggle between good and evil in IS's worldview. The enemies in this epic fight are those who do not submit to Allah's will (expressed in the proclaimed caliphate), and instead contribute to the oppression and discrimination of the few "true" believers. Remarkable is a peak (with 50 coded sense units) in the subcategory "wrong religion" in issue no. 5, which can be traced back to an interview with the "*Amir of Hisbah in Sinai*".

In many cases it is difficult to differentiate the category "*Delimitation to the majority*" clearly from the subcategory "*wrong religion*". Here passages are encoded that clearly delineate the followers of the IS and "their" Islam from the "majority Muslims". However, in this category this happens without building up an enemy image or calling for a fight against the other faiths of Islam. Considering the number of encoded 288 text passages, one can state, that this number exceeds the one of the above-mentioned subcategory. In most passages, distinctions of the majority of Islam and the delimitations of those as enemies alternated. An increase was found in the issues no. 7 – no. 9, since in these issues the establishment of the IS was justified with exactly this demarcation from the "majority Islam".

In the sense contexts of the category "*Clear rules*", almost every area of Muslims everyday life is set. From general social behavior to concrete instructions in specific situations. Often, these rules are extensively proved by Quran and Sunnah quotations, whereas others are established without theological justification. Often, rules are also implicitly formulated using the dichotomy of good-bad, just-disbelieving to express what values and norms of behavior prevail in IS. Another area within the rulebook are rules of jihadist behavior, the fight against the infidels, and dealing with enemies in combat, with jihad being a duty for all Muslims. Jihad includes the struggle in those states that are called the lands of the "disbelievers". Thus, the clear set of rules also includes recipients outside the territory occupied by the IS. In addition to direct guidelines, portrayals of punishments illustrate the consequences of breaking the rules. These punishments are often religiously justified. Some rules are aimed to specific target groups, who are assigned specific tasks within the world view of the IS. For example, women are called to serve their husbands faithfully and humbly, to support jihad by educating children and caring for the man.

In summary, the rules can be reduced to a few principles. Islam is a religion of war, requires *hijra* and *jihad*, and imposes the unconditional observance of *sharia* – as it is interpreted by the IS – in all public and private spheres. The correlation of the categories "*concept of the enemy*" and "*clear rules*" are in line with the radicalization theory. It shows the recipient, first and foremost solutions to personal crises and a simple explanation of the world. If they want to be on the "good side", they just must follow the rules offered, which are based on a radical interpretation of Islam. These are typical offers of the "*Orientation and Meaningfulness*", which occupies a much larger role, as the so called influential top category "*Social Relationship and Affiliation*" within radicalization models. The latter occurs more frequently if and only if the propaganda leaves the familiar pattern of "*concept of the enemy*" and "*clear rules*".

The category "*Supposed noble targets*" is closely related to the categories "*Superiority of IS*" and "*IS as Avantgard*". Here again and again the desired goals are derived from the religious mission of the "believers". Furthermore, the *Ummah* should be protected from oppression and external attacks (also related to the "*Deprivation*" category). Consequently, there are always focal points in the magazines, if there are sense contexts of those categories.

The main part of the category "*call for change and action*" are interviews and speeches, with direct calls for attacks in Western countries, calls to leave for the IS, or to turn back to "true" Islam. These calls are of utmost importance to Western state security agencies. Coupled with the instructions explaining in detail possible variants of terroristic attacks (view point 4.2.5), at a late stage of radicalization, passages of this category may lead one to the final deselection of an assassination. The peak in issue no. 5 is related to the presentation of arson attacks in which is repeatedly asked for carry out those. The peak in issue no. 11 is explained by the article "*Sisters, our Journey to Allah*" by asking young women to emigrate to the IS.

No sense units with the category "*adventure and borderline experience*" were encoded in the evaluated issues. This category was included in the analysis to allow comparability with the results from the secondary literature. However, when this category occurred, the focus of these sense units was in other categories - and according to Mayring, in quantitative content analysis, each sense unit can only be assigned to one category.

4.1.5 Uncoded sense units

The proportion of "*uncoded sense units*" varies between 27% and 51% in the respective editions. However, as already noted, these are text passages that cannot be subsumed under the formed category system. This does not mean that they can have not any influence on psychological processes - in the context of the radicalization process. A more detailed examination of these passages would be desirable and needed in the sense of holistic radicalization research.

4.2 Layout description

Examining the layout of the "*Rumiyah*" magazine was not the central point of my analysis work. Nevertheless, it is important to analyze the structure of the journal roughly, because it is common ground that the way in which content is prepared and presented influences the radicalization process. Especially for young people who are looking for alternative sources of information, conceptually well-thought-out journals like "*Rumiyah*" can offer an introduction to the Jihadist's world of topics and contribute to their radicalization (like stated by Brasher[112] and McFarlane[113]). The move to voluntary, self-contained "everyman terrorism" is putting new light on online self-radicalization processes, as they are not subject to chains of command or hierarchies.[114] In this context, individual types of below presented articles are playing an important role (under the heading "terror tactics").

4.2.1 Layout analysis design

The analysis of the layout was based on the same method as the content analysis. Inductively categories (here called "keyword") were built up for the individual articles. These keywords were used to quantitatively evaluate the layout. For each article, only one keyword was assigned, depending on the focus. In addition, an evaluation was carried out regarding the used pictures and their relation to the printed articles. A total of 10 keywords were assigned to categorize each content. Before the results are presented, the system of used keywords will be introduced:

Glorify CV – This Keyword includes glorifying CVs, from "heroes" and common fighters of the IS (additionally showing CV of suicide assassins) – anchor example article "*Among the Believers Are Men Abu Mansur al-Muhajir*"[115]

History – Presentation of historical events according to tradition (Hadith or Quran). Further the presentation of historical events and their interpretation from the point of IS's worldview are encoded here – anchor example article "*Sultan Mahmud Al-Ghaznawi*"[116]

Interview – Text in form of an interview in direct speech. The presentation takes place in question and answer (with name of the respective speaking one) – an-

---

[112] Brasher (2004)

[113] McFarlane (2011), online: <http://1dneox4dyqrx1207m11b46y7tfi.wpengine.netdna-cdn.com/r adicalisation/files/2013/03/>

[114] cf. Veilleux-Lapage (2014), online:
<https://www.academia.edu/9809988/_Retweeting_the_Cali phate_The_Role_of_Soft-Sympathizers_in_the_Islamic_State_s_Social_Media_Strategy_Paper_ present-ed_at_the_6th_International_Symposium_on_Terrorism_and_Transnational_Crime_in_Antalya_Turkey>

[115] N.N., *supra* note 75, p. 14ff

[116] N.N., *supra* note 75, p. 36ff

chor example article *"Interview with the Amir of the Central office for investigating grievances"*[117]

Propaganda promotion – Direct advertising for the download of videos, apps, etc. which are distributed by the IS or a related organization in the world wide web – anchor example article *"Selected 10 Videos From The Wilayat Of The Islamic State"*[118]

Religion – Reports with a centrally religious background. These include, on the one hand, the theological justification for different behaviors and the theological background to the construction of IS. Also included are reports that show a theological delineation from the moderate currents of Islam – anchor example article *"The Religion of Islam And the Jama'ah of the Muslims"*[119]

Report – This keyword was given for reports from everyday life within IS, as well as, for example, the presentation of political events outside the IS. It has also been used to encode texts that disseminate "general knowledge" in the sense of the ideology of IS – anchor example article *"Stand and Die Upon That for Which Your Brothers Died"*[120]

Speech – The summary or transcribed presentation of speeches that have been made by clergy or responsible persons of IS – anchor example article *"This is what Allah and his Messenger promised us"*[121]

Successes – Under this keyword representations of successes are subsumed. The presentation can take the form of a text or a graphic – anchor example article *"Military and Covert Operations"*[122]

Terror tactics – This keyword includes articles, that describe terror tactics and thus animate for imitations (approach, advantages, disadvantages, ...) – anchor example article *"Just Terror Tactics"*[123]

---

[117] N.N., *supra* note 75

[118] *ibid.*, p. 9

[119] N.N., *supra* note 79, p. 14ff

[120] N.N., *supra* note 75, p. 2f

[121] N.N., *supra* note 77, p. 4ff

[122] N.N., *supra* note 79, p. 34ff

[123] N.N., *supra* note 75, p. 12f

Title – This keyword contains the title page, back cover and the table of contents – title, back cover one can see in every issue, additionally the table of contend started in issue no. 7 (the presentation of an anchor example was omitted in this case).

The analysis-datasheets in detail can be viewed in the appendix, point 11.4.2.

4.2.2 General findings

In general, it can be stated that various articles glorify the IS fighters – at the same time they portray IS's successes in a pathetic way. Throw this medialization and popularization of the struggle a cult of martyrdom shall be built up. Again, and again, clear differences between the "commonplace Islam" and the "right Islam" disseminated by IS are presented. In addition, the magazine highlights one aspect – that Western media coverage hardly addresses – namely, everydayness and (supposed) normality. Beyond the reports of atrocities, war, death and attacks, these Western journalists show little interest in the banal daily life in the IS. Quite differently, a significant amount of *"Rumiyah"* content presents the seemingly normal life in the proclaimed caliphate. This can be actively used in the sense of recruiting followers, as Awan[124] found in his research about the jihadist internet media work. Because the absence of these contents in the mass media consider supporters and sympathizers of the IS as confirmation for a one-sided and discriminating reporting. This perception leads to the further development of the view, separating the "we" from the "others".

Before entering the analysis representation, it can be determined first that the total number of pages of the magazine varies from issue to issue. The thinnest issues have 38 pages, the thickest 60. Correspondingly, the thicker edition contains more encoded contents and pictures.

4.2.3 Quantity of content

The number of articles encoded with a keyword varies from 16 to 21. It should be noted that there is no significant conspicuousness. On average, the articles have a length of 2.0 to 2.4 pages. Looking at the proportions of the various contents by keyword, it is noticeable that the areas of *religion*, *report* and *successes* provide the bulk of the content.

---

[124] Awan (2016)

Keyword	Σ pages with keyword content
glorify CV	26
history	24.5
interview	30
propaganda promotion	22.5
religion	168
report	167
speech	26
successes	74
terror tactics	19
title	33
total Σ pages	590

Figure 5: Layout analysis – table of pages with keyword content

All issues of the "*Rumiyah*" magazine have a cover and a back cover. As of issue no. 7, the table of contents was added as a separate page. On the cover page is always the number of the issue, as well as the date of publication in the Islamic calendar. Behind the title "*Rumiyah*" is an abbreviation that indicates the printed language. On the cover of the first 6 issues, or. on the page of the table of contents from issue no. 7 on, there is the citation:

"O muwahhidin, rejoice, for by Allah, we will not rest from our jihad except beneath the olive trees of Rumiyah (Rome)"

– which is supposed to be the long-term goal of the IS. From issue no. 7 on the cover page has a subtitle.

In each issue, articles about *religion* are playing a major role. Considering the total number of all the whole content, as well as the whole number of pages, it occupies the first place. There is an accumulation of religious articles through issues no. 7 to no. 9. This is because issue no. 7 shed light on the establishing of the IS. In the issues no. 7 to no. 9 religious reasons for the founding of the state, as well as religious rules of conduct for the everyday life and clear demarcations from other faiths of the Islam were printed increased. Articles coded as *report* are available in every issue and rank second behind religious ones. It's a mix of articles, some of them from everyday life at the IS to reports of fighting for the cities of Mosul or Raqqah.

An integral part of each issue is a presentation of IS's own *successes*. For this there is a separate section which changed its name and layout during the published issues. In Issue no. 1 and no. 2, the series is called *"Operations"*, from issue no. 3 on *"Military and Covert Operations"*. This renaming was supposed to substantiate the fact that the IS fighters not only fight on the fronts of the war zone, but also carry out covert operations in the countries of "disbelievers". Regarding the change in the corresponding background image, reference is made to point 4.2.4.

Speeches by official spokesmen of IS in direct speech or in summary occur only in four issues. These are marked by appeals to the followers, concepts of enemy and clear delimitations from other religious currents within Islam. Content coded as *glorify CV* does not appear in every issue. However, if content in this category occurs, it can be found, that relatively large amount of space is given to them from the authors. These are mainly reports of martyrs in the sense of IS, or suicide bombers. *History* articles appeared in issue no. 3 till no. 7 and no. 10, so they were not available in every issue. *Interviews* with executives within IS, printed in verbal speech with questions and answers, occurred in seven of the 13 issues. The aim of these articles was mostly the representation of the superiority of IS's fighters and the representation of the just cause for IS's fight. The area of *propaganda and promotion* includes concrete advertising pages for videos, apps and other media produced by IS for sympathizers and supporters. Mainly is advertised for videos produced by Al-Hayat and distributed on YouTube. It is noteworthy that also for apps programmed for PC and Android devices is advertised, which include religious teachings (in the sense of IS) that is targeted to children (tailored age appropriate). There is advertising for brochures, too, containing collections of reports from Islamist fanzines.

Concerning the contents coded as *terror and tactics*, reference is made to the separate presentation under point 4.2.5..

4.2.4 Quantity of pictures

For the analysis of the printed 562 pictures, these were counted quantitatively by assignment to the above-mentioned keywords (used graphics were counted like pictures). A direct comparison of the total number of pictures among the individual issues is not expedient since the page numbers vary as described. For this reason, a frequency number of pictures has been constructed, extrapolated to 100 pages for each issue – now a comparison is possible:

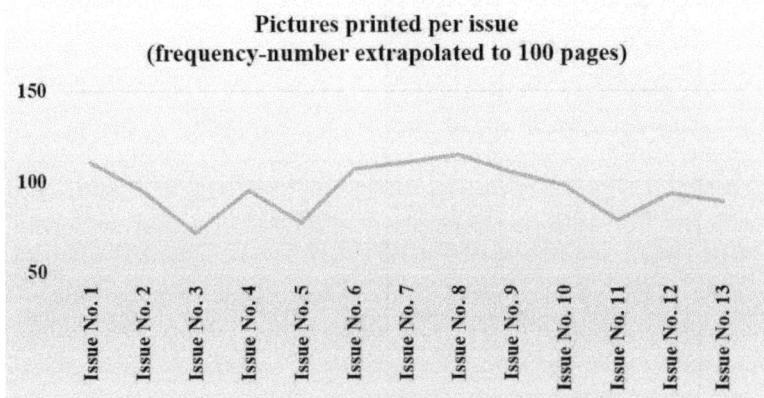

Figure 6: Layout analysis chart – frequency-number pictures per issue

In the graph is no individual peak noticeable. Nor could it be determined that the number of pictures increased or decreased linearly as issues progressed. It can be assumed that the authors of the IS consciously use pictures. During analyzing the *"Rumiyah"* magazine issues – in context of the relationship between text and pictures – I can state, that clearly text outweighs. Seemingly other communication platforms such as YouTube or Twitter are used by IS as a medium for excessive dissemination of pictures, but not this magazine.

It can be stated that the magazines rarely show pictures of executions or disfigured bodies. Rather, the pictures are pictures of IS fighters in heroic poses, praying IS fighters on battlefields, pictures of everyday life, or crying, sad soldiers of the West and their allies.

Keyword	Σ pictures per keyword
glorify CV	21
history	17
religion	129
report	120
speech	17
successes	82
terror tactics	24
title	51
propaganda promotion	78
interview	23
total Σ pictures	562

Figure 7: Layout analysis – table of pictures per keyword

Considered quantitatively in detail, it can be determined that pictures from the encoded area of *religion* and *report* represent most of the pictures used. The part of *successes* is also underpinned with a variety of images. The reason for the high number of pictures in the field of *propaganda and promotion* is because the advertising pages usually present online videos (there are always several pictures from the video sequences displayed on one side of the magazine).

Particularly striking in the analysis work was the change in the background image[125] in the ongoing series of articles *"Operations"* (later *"Military and Covert Operations"*), in which the successes of the IS were presented. Especially this series with a fixed place in each issue has a kind of recognition value and nevertheless, a change was introduced here. In issue no. 1 and no. 2, the report has got the title *"Operations"* – from issue no. 3 on, the title is *"Military and Covert Operations"*. From issue no. 1 until finally no. 7, in the background image one can see a map of the world with implied impacts all around the world; above one can see a group of fighters with weapons and carrying masks. In issue no. 8 and no. 9, above the map there is a group of fighters who fight under IS's banner. From issue no. 10 on,

---

[125] view appendix, point 11.4.3

above the map one can see a platoon of uniform wearing IS fighters proudly stay-
ing under two IS's banners. Through this change in self-presentation, the authors
of the magazine attempt to portray the shift from a group of unconventional fighters to a conventional army fighting for IS – on battlefields and covert all around
the world (which every opponent must take seriously).

4.2.5 "Manuals" for terror tactics

One aim of *"Ruminyah"* magazine's authors is, inter alia, to introduce the reader
the above-mentioned self-made "every man" terrorism tactics. They shall not only
be informed about advantages and disadvantages of different types of terror attacks, but they will be given a precise description of possible procedures – like a
manual for lone wolf terrorism. From state security authorities' point of view,
these articles should be evaluated in detail and the underlying tactical action routines should be analyzed. Thus, operational intervention concepts can be optimized for cases of terrorism attacks and human lives possibly saved. In the context of my master thesis no analysis of these articles takes place in detail, they are
only presented here briefly:

Issue 1: "The Kafir's blood is halal for you, so shed it"[126]

This report explains to the readers why it is not only necessary, but even explicitly
allowed to kill disbelievers everywhere and at any time. The article calls directly
for the execution of terrorism attacks worldwide. Here are no concrete procedures or recommendations for weapons used.

Issue 2: "Just Terror Tactics – Knife attacks"[127]

In this report, the knife is presented as a suitable weapon for terrorist attacks
committed by lone wolves. It explains what is important to know for the choice of
knife, for the way how to cut or stab, for the choice of the victim, and for the
choice of right place. The after-attack behavior is also described (with exemplary
presentation of how confession to assassinations can be done).

---

[126] N.N., *supra* note 75, p. 34ff
[127] N.N., *supra* note 82, p. 12f

Issue 3: "Just Terror Tactics – Vehicle attacks"[128]

The focus of this report is the presentation of suitable vehicles for perpetration of a vehicle attack. It explains how one could seize vehicles best, which targets are to be chosen, how to commit the assault, and how to behave after the attack (among other things, if one is not able to continue driving, the killing should be continued by foot by use of hand weapons).

Issue 4: "*Knife Attacks*"[129]

Short summary of the article from issue 2 – on one page, with many pictures, graphics and schemas.

Issue 5: "*Just Terror Tactics – Arson Attacks*"[130]

Explanations what to consider in an arson attack. The report contains detailed instructions on how to assemble a Molotov cocktail and how to use it best. It also explains exactly, what to look for, during choosing a target.

Issue 9: "*Just Terror Tactics – Hostage Taking*"[131]

Manual on how to prepare a hostage-taking best; what must be considered during execution (armament, number of perpetrators, etc.), which locations are best suited, how to gather as many victims as possible in one place, and which countermeasures can be expected from the security forces. It is important to notice that according to this manual, the goal of the hostage-takers is not to make demands, but to receive the greatest possible media attention and then spread terror by killing as many people as possible – a negotiated solution is not an option in such hostage situations for security forces!

Issue 9: "*Just Terror Tactics – Truck attacks*"[132]

Short summary of the article from issue 3 – on one page, with many pictures, graphics and schemas.

In general, it can be stated that the authors place a noticeable emphasis in their reports on after-attack behavior. It is always explained how a presumed perpetra-

---

[128] N.N., *supra* note 80, p. 10ff

[129] N.N., *supra* note 1, p. 8

[130] N.N., *supra* note 76, p. 8ff

[131] N.N. (2017c), online: <https://jihadology.net/category/rome-magazine/>, p. 46ff

[132] *ibid.*, p. 56

tor after the attack can proclaim the deed for himself best (of course in the name of IS). Additionally, great emphasis is placed on how the deeds can best be marketed medially.

4.3 Interim conclusion

Overall, 13 issues of the *"Ruminyah"* magazine were analyzed in terms of content and layout, a total of 590 pages of research material. The texts were divided into 3.939 sense units (additionally 562 pictures). Generally, it can be stated, that 40.92% of the sense units were uncoded ones, the 59.08% of the encoded area can be broken down as follows: a share of 35.26% is summed up to the main category *"Orientation and Meaningfulness"*, 21.06% under the main category *"Social Relationship and Affiliation"*, and 1.85% under the main category *"Deprivation"*.

The main category *"Deprivation"* represents the smallest share of the main categories. This main category deals with the portrayal of the global victimhood of Sunni Muslims (the *Ummah*), who are opposed and oppressed by the West and his allies – IS describes itself as the only legitimate savior for the *Ummah*. In summary, however, the authors of the *"Ruminayh"* magazine obviously did not make *"Deprivation"* to a priority topic of their journal. Nevertheless, form the point of view of radicalization research, it is an important part of content, which can strongly influence radicalization processes.

Within the main category *"Social relationship and Affiliation"* the category *"Achievment of IS"* dominates with a total share of 13.35%. Presenting IS's successes is an integral part of each *"Ruminayh"* issue. In the early issues the authors directly refer to territorial expansions of the area of influence, later more and more smaller successes and results of terroristic assassinations worldwide are presented. By naming its achievements, IS constructs an output legitimacy as genuine state or caliphate. Through the presentation of the successes, the superiority of the IS, the self-called avant-garde among the jihadist groups, is staged. The contents subsumed under the categories *"Superiority of IS"* and *"IS as Avantgarde"* range continuously at the same level, with a direct dependency to the presentations of the *"Achievment of IS"*. These two categories consistently contain positive self-description of the IS – further they deal with description as a currently unique and historical phenomenon whose existence is due to direct will of Allah (literally seen the IS's followers are called as a superior conspiratorial community). Only a small share of sense units can be counted to the category *"Social*

Security" – the focus of *"Ruminayh"* contents in connection with the main category *"Social Relationship and Affiliation"* is on above named three other categories.

The largest share with 35.26% of the whole sense units represents the encoded part of the main category *"Orientation and Meaningfulness"*. The category *"Concept of the enemy"* leads in this share with 11.98%. The categories *"clear rules"*, *"supposed noble targets"*, and *"Delimitation to the majority"* move nearly at the same level – between 5.33% and 7.31%. *"Call for change and action"* with 3.94% is the smallest countable share.

"Concept of the enemy" is divided into the three subcategories *"wrong religion"*, *"the West and Allies"*, and *"other jihadist groups"*. Whereby the first two subcategories build up the bigger part with 5.59% and 6.02%. Generally, the IS tries to explain the justification for their fight against the rest of the world by creating a clear demarcation – a friend / enemy Dichotomy. This concept of enemies contains not only the Western countries and their allies in the middle East – other faiths of Islam are repeatedly led into the field, too. Even if with only a small proportion (0.38%), there is a clear demarcation from other jihadist groups, because the IS proclaims the monopoly for a just jihad in defense of the Muslim world only for itself.

It is difficult to differentiate the category *"Delimitation to the majority"* clearly from the subcategory *"wrong religion"* in many cases. In the most passages distinctions of the majority of Islam and the delimitations of those as enemies alternated (there is a concrete correlation).

In summary, the *"clear rules"* (share of 6.7%) can be reduced to a few principles. Islam is a religion of war, requires *hijra* and *jihad*, and imposes the unconditional observance of *sharia* – as it is interpreted by IS – in all public and private spheres. The correlation of the categories *"concept of the enemy"* and *"clear rules"* are in line with the radicalization theory. It shows the recipient, first and foremost solutions to personal crises and a simple explanation of the world. If they want to be on the "good side", they just have to follow the offered rules – if one does not accept or breaks the rules, he will be counted to the enemy.

"Supposed noble targets" (share of 6.7%) are justified on the one hand by the religious mission to the superior community of the IS and on the other hand by the suffered deprivation.

For Western security agencies the category *"call for change and action"* are for utmost importance. Because here the IS calls directly for terroristic attacks in the

Western countries and animates recipients to emigrate to IS's occupied land-scapes.

No sense units were given the category *"adventure and borderline experience"*, since if they were considered for the categorization, usually they stepped back behind the main meaning in the sense units.

The proportion of *"uncoded sense units"* (in meaning of the used category system) varies between 27 and 51%. This does not mean that they can have not any influence on psychological processes – in context of the radicalization process (detailed examinations of these passages would be desirable and needed in the sense of holistic radicalization research).

It is common ground, that the way in which content is prepared and presented to recipients influences the radicalization process. For this reason, the Layout was analyzed. In general, it can be stated, that the used Layout tries to underline the aims of IS – glorify IS's fighters, building up a cult of martyrdom, delimitation IS's Islam of "commonplace" Islam, and depiction of the normality of everyday life. The number of pages varies per issue from 38 to 60. On average, the articles have a length of 2.0 till 2.4 pages. Looking at the proportions of the various contents by keyword, the areas of *religion, report* and *successes* rule. The professionalization of the layout while the issues is reflected in the insertion of a table of contents from issue no. 7 onwards. Noteworthy is the area of *"propaganda and promotion"* produced by Al-Hayat, advertising not only videos, magazines and books. Among other there is a targeted advertising for apps programmed for PC and Android devices, which include religious teachings (in sense of IS) that is targeted to children (tailored age appropriate). The quantitatively analyzation of the printed 562 picture gave the same result as the content layout analysis – pictures with the keyword *religion, report* and *successes* rule. The frequency number of pictures up to 100 pages per issue has no individual noticeable peak. It can be stated that the magazines rarely show pictures of executions or disfigured bodies. Rather, the pictures are pictures of IS fighters in heroic poses, praying IS fighters on battle-fields, pictures of everyday life, or crying, sad soldiers of the West and their allies.

The example of the background image of the series "Operations" (later "Military and Covert Operations") shows the attempt of the IS, to show the shift from a group of unconventional fighters to a conventional army fighting for IS - on battle-fields and covert all around the world (which every enemy must take seriously).

In issues no. 1, no. 2, no. 3, no. 4, no. 5, and no. 9 "manuals" for terror tactics were printed. They reach form knife attacks, vehicle attacks, over arson attacks to hostage tacking. Recipients shall not only be informed about advantages and disadvantages of different types of terror attacks, but they will be given a precise description of possible procedures – like a manual for lone wolf terrorism, that can be executed everywhere and at any time. From state security authorities' point of view, these articles should be evaluated in detail and the underlying tactical action routines should be analyzed. Thus, operational intervention concepts can be optimized for cases of terrorism attacks and human lives possibly saved.

5 Comparison with the findings about the "DABIQ" magazine

5.1 Comparison of content analysis findings

Since my performed content analysis based on identical criteria as the analysis of Kiefer et. al of the "*Dabiq*" magazine in 2017,[133] the results[134] are comparable.

Code rules	"Dabiq" Σ total in %	"Rumiyah" Σ total in %
Deprivation	6,77%	1,85%
Social Relationship and Affiliation	18,30%	21,96%
Orientation and Meaningfulness	33,85%	35,26%
Uncoded Sense Units	41,09%	40,92%
	100,00%	100,00%

Figure 8: Comparison analyzes results "Dabiq" vs. "Rumiyah"

In principle, it can be noted that the distribution of the individual shares has remained the same in terms of size in both journals. The area of "*Deprivation*" was the smallest in both journals and the area "*Orientation and Meaningfulness*" the largest. The percentage breakdown differs only slightly, except in the main category of "*Deprivation*". The share of the "*uncoded sense units*" is with round about 41% nearly the same. If the categories below the main categories are compared in detail, the following can be stated:

- The "*Achievment of IS*" category in the "*Rumiyah*" magazine is almost twice as common as in its predecessor (6.41% to 13.35%).

- IS does not advertise as often with the factor "*Social Security*" as before (2.77% to 0.18%).

- The dictation of "*clear rules*" is not so frequent in the texts as in the past (10.01% to 6.70%).

- In the "*concept of the enemy*" category, a shift in the concept, away from "*other jihadist groups*" (6.13% to 0.38%) towards "*wrong religion*" (3.46% to 5.59%), took place.

---

[133] Kiefer et al., *supra* note 29

[134] a detailed comparison of the results of both content analysis can be found in the Appendix (Point 11.4.4)

- Much more "*supposed noble targets*" (1.33% to 5.33%) are used in the propaganda now.

- The advertisement with "*Adventure and borderline experience*" disappeared (2.75% to 0.00%)

- Now one of the most important aims of IS is the "*Delimitation of the majority*" of the other faiths of Islam (0.64% to 7.31%).

The two main differences in content between the two magazines are:

- In the "*Ruminyah*" magazine is increasingly advertised for the *jihad* in Western countries. In the framework of the "*Dabiq*" magazine, attempts were made to persuade as many recipients as possible to emigrate to the territory of the IS – now efforts are being made to carry out *jihad* into countries all over the world. IS's aim is to spread fear among the "disbelievers" in their home countries. In view of the ever-increasing area losses of the IS, this statement coincides with the call away from the *hijrah* to the *jihad* in the western countries.

- The very differentiated concept of the enemy of the "*Dabiq*" magazine changes now in a more general, so that individual hostile jihadist groups in the "*Rumiyah*" magazine are almost not mentioned. IS tries to present the war as one between "good and evil", "true and false" religion.

Overall, the changed political situation of the IS can be seen in its used propaganda, too.

5.2 Comparison of layout analysis findings

There are no layout analyses of the "*Dabiq*" nor the "*Ruminyah*" magazine in the secondary literature that can be compared methodically with my own. For this reason, the rare results of other comparative investigations must be used here. Generally, Spada points to similarities between the two magazines in layout, photographic style and appeal to a Western audience.[135] Pragalath stated that "*Rumiyah*" is said to be made up of articles which have been recycled from IS's daily news bulletins while "*Dabiq*" featured new content. Additionally, "*Rumiyah*" focuses more on current operations, while its predecessor emphasizes longer-term

---

[135] cf. Spada (2016), online: <http://www.islamedianalysis.info/rumiyah-the-new-islamic-state-mag azine-glosses-over-reality-of-caliphate/>

goals and on propagating IS ideology.[136] Similarly, Friedland points to differences, stating that IS has switched away from *"Dabiq"* in favor of an easier to read, less theological magazine.[137]

5.3 Interim conclusion

After comparing the content of the two magazines can be stated that, the distribution of the individual shares of the sense units encoded in the main categories remained nearly the same in terms of size in both journals. The largest share is the one of *"Orientation and Meaningfulness"*, the smallest one is *"Deprivation"*. The share of the *"uncoded sense units"* in both magazines is 41%. There are two main points striking difference in content: Firstly, in the *"Ruminyah"* magazine is increasingly advertised for the jihad in Western countries aimed to spread terror and threat over there. In the *"Dabiq"* magazine the focus was on the call to the recipients to emigrate to the IS. Secondly, the differentiated concept of the enemy of the *"Dabiq"* magazine changed in a more general – IS tries now to present their war as one between the "good and the evil", "true and false" religion.

In the absence of comparable layout analysis in the secondary literature, only the following general comparative statements can be made: With regard to the general layout, the photographic style and appeal to Western audience, the two magazines are very similar. *"Ruminyah"* recycles articles from IS's daily news bulletin (with the focus on current operations) while *"Dabiq"* featured new content (with focus on longer-term goals and IS ideology). Additionally, *"Rumiyah"* is written easier to read for the recipients and has less theological content.

---

[136] cf. Pragalath (2016), online: <https://www.beritadaily.com/rumiyah-would-not-replace-dabiq/>

[137] cf. Friedland (2016), online: <https://clarionproject.org/latest-issue-isis-rumiyah-magazine-released/>

6 Possible counter measures

6.1 Possible measures against online propaganda

In context of this master thesis I showed how IS (using the content of the journal *"Rumiyah"*) tries to recruit new followers in the Internet and tries to radicalize them afterwards. At this point, I will present two possible solutions to a question that has already occupied many academics, governments and civil society actors alike: How do we deal with the accompanying dangers of this dark side of internet freedoms?[138] Of course, this question cannot be conclusively discussed in scope of this thesis - therefore, this chapter is only to be seen as a description of the problem and rough outline of possible solutions in context.

However, one solution possibility in those cases is the generally deletion of contents or the deactivation of IS-supporting user accounts and web pages. The most discussed initiative in the German context for this is the Netzwerk-durchsuchungsgesetz (NetzDG).[139] The benefits of this law are certainly evident. With the help of this law, one can theoretically deliberately contain the spread of Islamist propaganda and thus prevent the way into Islamism. In addition, the contact of IS forces for online recruitment would be more difficult, if user accounts are deleted in case of repeated violations against network guidelines.

At the same time, the effectiveness of this law is not foreseeable and, especially in the context of IS's online approach, its effectiveness is questionable. IS spreads its propaganda not only by one account – they usually use a large network of supporters who share the critical contents. De facto, it all boils down to a competition between IS supporters and the deletion mechanisms of social networks – with an open end. Furthermore, a broad resistance against the adopted NetzDG has been formed in Germany as well as internationally. The legality of the law is questioned

---

[138] cf. Pohjonen & Ahmed (2016), p. 236

[139] Above all, the NetzDG is discussed in the public, because of its effects on the topic of "fake news" and "hate speech". In fact, the law adopted on June 30th, 2017, is directed against criminal offenses such like § 86 StGB (spread of propaganda of unconstitutional organizations). Therefore, the promulgation of propaganda on behalf of the IS (which is prohibited since September 2014 unopposed by the Federal Interior Ministry) must be subsumed under this law. The current version of this law can be accessed in different languages at the following internet address:
<https://www.bmjv.de/SharedDocs/Gesetzgebungsverfahren/DE/NetzDG.html>; accessed 12June 2018)

by various parties. For example, the Göttingen Professor of Internet Law Spindler (in his report commissioned by the IT industry association *"Bitkom"*) found that the provisions of the law violated certain personal rights. One example mentioned by him is the violation of Article 4 (II) of the EU Data Protection Directive.[140] The UN Special Representative on the Promotion and Protection of Freedom of Expression Kaye, has also criticized in his letter to the German government various points in this law. He points out, inter alia, that according to the expert opinions of the UN Human Rights Council (A/HRC17/31 and A/HRC/32/38), the responsibility of censorship measures may not be passed on to private actors. States could also not require these private actors to unjustifiably and unreasonably restrict freedom of expression. Furthermore, the law violates various provisions of the international covenant on civil and political rights.[141]

Another prominent claim frequently made following terrorist attacks relates to end-to-end encryption of various messenger services. Sometimes these are used to send messages to recruit and schedule attacks. Especially "Telegram" is focused by governmental agencies, because it is a favored medium used by terrorist organizations in several cases. In the context of these public discussions, it is repeatedly demanded that such messenger services should incorporate a backdoor into their programs. This would allow security agencies to decode private encrypted messages. Markus Ra, a kind of press spokesman[142] for "Telegram", has pointed out in an open letter with the clear title "Don't shoot the messenger" that such a backdoor cannot only be made accessible to governments and law enforcement agencies. As soon as such a possibility is opened, sooner or later extremist groups and hackers could find that gap, too. He also notes that terrorist groups would, if necessary, develop their own messenger services, since the needed encryption keys would be freely accessible on the Internet. These group-

---

[140] cf. Spindler (2017), online: <https://www.bitkom.org/Bitkom/Publikationen/Gutachten-von-Prof-Dr-Gerald-Spindler-zum-Netzwerkdurchsetzungsgesetz.html>

[141] cf. Kaye (2017), online:
<https://www.ohchr.org/Documents/Issues/Opinion/Legislation/OL-DEU-1-2017.pdf>

[142] There is almost no reliable information about the company structure of "Telegram". Ra is one of a palmful of people who have ever made public statements in the name of this company. He calls himself "head of support, media and whatever" (view homepage of "Telegram": <https://core.telegram.org/tsi>; accessed 12June 2018).

ings could also use alternative communication channels or simply use coded language.[143]

Overall, it can be stated that measures such as deliberate deletion of accounts and content or the decryption of messages are controversial discussed in terms of their impact and legality. All of these measures are part of the major ethical debate on the tension between freedom and security, too. (Is anyone willing to increase his own safety by allowing more surveillance? Or does the opposite position stand in the way – cannot an increase in security be achieved simply by expanding surveillance? Could not more security theoretically lead to more freedom?)

The second, very prominent intervention measure against the effects of online propaganda, is the use of so-called *"counter-narratives"*. This means

> "[...] a message that offers a positive alternative to extremist propaganda, or alternatively aims to deconstruct or delegitimize extremist narratives."[144]

Braddock and Horgan[145] have proposed the following content criteria:

> "[...] revealing incongruities and contradictions in the terrorist narratives and how terrorists act, disrupting analogies between the target narrative and real-world events, disrupting binary themes of the group's ideology, and advocating an alternative view of the terrorist narrative's target [...]"[146]

Ingram and Read recommend that you stylistically work with a large main narrative supported by multiple customizable narratives – instead of treating each case individually and constantly developing new small-scale narratives.[147] Such actions could lead to incredibility. In addition, the use of various types of message types is recommended. On the one hand, messages should be used that focus rational arguments, on the other hand, those that are more emotional in nature. A balanced mix of proactive spread narratives and defensive narratives responding to other

---

[143] cf. Ra (2017), online: <http://telegra.ph/Dont-shoot-the-messenger>

[144] cf. Amanullah et al. (2016), online: <https://www.isdglobal.org/wp-content/uploads/2016/08/Im pact-of-Counter-Narratives_ONLINE_1.pdf>

[145] cf. Braddock & Horgan (2015)

[146] cf. *ibid.*, p. 397

[147] cf. Ingram & Reed, *supra* note 43

online entries should be found.[148] Lieberman suggests using credible multipliers and communicators in disseminating counter-narratives.[149] Ideally, these interpretations are disseminated by ex-IS militants or people around them. By doing that way, there is a great chance to achieve the highest possible credibility. It should be avoided that state actors spread these narratives, because this could give the impression of indoctrination. At this point I would like to introduce two initiatives by way of example – *"The ISIS Defectors Interviews Project"* and the *"Sakinah-Project"*.

"The ISIS Defectors Interviews Project" uses the concept of counter narratives applied by IS returnees. They produced 43 videoclips, which should serve as a counterweight to Islamist propaganda. These clips are uploaded on video sharing platforms, that tend to be used for Islamist recruiting, or directly on the online presence of IS supporters. Additionally, they are tagged with keywords and hashtags usually used by these group of people. Currently this project is still in its infancy; the first pretests started last year.[150]

One step further is already the *"Sakinah-Project"* started in Saudi Arabia. This project started in 2003. Scientists in a variety of disciplines are trying to confront people, who propagate extremist ideology online, with more moderate interpretations of Islam. In the context of this confrontation special legal or theological questions are discussed in religious framework. In the current project interim report 3250 confrontations were recorded, of which approximately 1500 are considered successful[151] in the sense of the project.[152]

During the analysis work on the *"Ruminyah"* magazine I stumbled upon the following passage, which shows that the propaganda machine of the IS is aware of and even fears the danger of counter-narratives:

---

[148] cf. *ibid.*

[149] cf. Liberman (2017), p. 120

[150] cf. McDowell-Smith, Speckhard & Yayla (2017), online:
<http://journals.sfu.ca/jd/index.php/jd /article/view/83>, pp. 50–76

[151] Which indicators they use to classify a confrontation as "successful in sense of the project", however, is not more precisely defined in this report.

[152] cf. Al-Saud (2017), p. 59f

"[...] Indeed, the blazing missiles of media are more lethal and more dangerous for the Ummah and its men, than the infernal missiles fired from warplanes. [...]"[153]

Even the concept of counter-narrative is criticized by several authorities – Glazzard[154] states that the idea of counter-narrative comes primarily from the ranks of governments and civil society. There are hardly any theoretical concepts or empirical findings on this theme. In his opinion, the scarce resources should not be used exclusively for those projects – as long as the effect has not been sufficiently researched.[155] Add to that the danger of the so-called *"backfire effect"*, as Kaspar[156] critically notes on the online blog on security studies at the University of Leiden. According to this effect, an immunization against criticism can be observed in people already convinced by a topic. In this case counter narratives would not lead to a rethinking, but rather strengthen the already existing opinion.

The listed criticisms show that there is disagreement over the effects and effectiveness of these measures in the extremist context. Several questions remain open: Can counter narratives really have sustainable success? How to measure causal success? Can these narratives be applied to people who are already highly radicalized and who stand shorty before an act? The issue of appropriate countermeasures against Islamist online propaganda is a major challenge for governments, civil society and science alike.

6.2 Possible offline measures after radicalization (deradicalization)

In recent years deradicalization has become an inflationary term without a satisfactory definition.[157] The differentiation to preventive work is sometimes not stringent, and the transitions between preventive approaches can be fluid. Of course, each definition depends on the anticipatory framing of the concept. So far, scientists and experts agree only relatively little: Radicalization is a process that is determined by many different factors;[158] there are many paths into radical scenes,

---

[153] N.N. (2017b), online: <https://jihadology.net/category/rome-magazine/>, p. 23

[154] cf. Glazzard (2017)

[155] cf. *ibid.*, p. 3f

[156] cf. Kasper (2017), online: <http://www.leidensafetyandsecurityblog.nl/articles/counter-narrative s-and-the-backfire-effect>

[157] cf. Horgan (2010), p. 3

[158] cf. Schmid (2013), online: <https://www.icct.nl/download/file/ICCT-Schmid-Radicalisation-De-Radicalisation-Counter-Radicalisation-March-2013_2.pdf>, p. 1

and the influencing factors of this process can be very different.[159] For this purpose, one could derive in advance important theses for the definition and conceptualization of the way how to handle deradicalization: First, deradicalization measures should also be understood as a process; secondly, this process will be different for each person concerned and, thirdly, any approaches and programs that work on these phenomena should therefore also be individualized.

According to the broad definition of John Horgan, deradicalization work means programs that are generally geared toward radicalized individuals, with the aim of reintegrating them into society, or at least dissuading them from direct (physical) violence.[160] However, deradicalization should not be misinterpreted as a reduction that immediately turns former terrorists into model democrats.[161] Unlike most preventive approaches, it is usually about working with individuals. Approaches can take different forms, inter alia: intervention (for persons who are about to join radical groups); exit-programs; collective deradicalization programs (group work); counseling with individuals (e.g. in prisons) or secondary deradicalization work (in which the focus is on the social environment of the person concerned).

In attempting to offer a precise and operationalizable definition of deradicalization, the distinction between deradicalization and disengagement must be made.[162] Deradicalization is usually understood as the cognitive rejection of certain extremist values, actions and opinions.[163] Disengagement means when a person renounces violent acts or an extremist group. However, disengagement does not mean equal deradicalization. The fact a person does not explicitly identify with the violent (militant) Islamist scene does not necessarily mean that a critical ideological confrontation (i.e., deradicalization in the true sense) has taken place. In addition, disengagement can also be unplanned for a variety of reasons, i.e. without targeted intervention, such as through dreams, stress, de-illusion, desire for a normal life.[164]

---

[159] cf. Christmann, *supra* note 27

[160] cf. Institute for Strategic Dialogue (2010), online: <http://bit.ly/24B5ceX>, p. 4f

[161] cf. Taken & Kevenhörster (2012), p. 212

[162] cf. Horgan, *supra* note 158, p. 3

[163] cf. Schmid, *supra* note 159

[164] cf. *ibid.*, p. 44

In this regard, it is essential to consider and question what exactly the aim of de-radicalization work is:

Is the focus on preventing fundamentalist Salafists from engaging in acts of violence, regardless of which ideologies or partial ideologies they still represent (disengagement), or in order to facilitate ideological and religious confrontation, so that the individuals concerned with their worldviews and attitudes to become (re-) integrable in a participatory democracy of liberal character?[165]

In the following, the emphasis is on deradicalization, without neglecting the approaches of disengaging. Depending on the objective, the measures of different groups of actors differ. If the focus is exclusively on security-related issues, as is often the case with state institutions and programs, then distancing may be extremely sensible from the point of view of countering terrorism.

But if it is also about the treatment of anti-democratic phenomena, an ideological deradicalization should involve more than a mere distancing from violence. The intensity of the work differs in practice regarding the desired goal as well as the persons and support structures to be included.

The goal definition of what is called deradicalization is the foundation for working with those affected. This definition depends on the respective context of implementation, the target group and the implementing authority (e.g. deradicalization programs in prisons, state offers, religious programs, sociological and psychological approaches, civil society activities and associations, etc.).[166]

Like in the case of prevention, there are few reliable empirical data on the effectiveness of deradicalization measures.[167] Firstly, this is because the success of deradicalization programs is difficult to measure. Often, for example, one starts from the recidivism rate, which only concerns the distancing of criminal behavior.[168] Secondly, like Horgan points out, terrorists usually become uninteresting to the state as soon as they are no longer viewed as a threat.[169] From then on, their case will no longer be followed up and further explored. This has the consequence that

---

[165] cf. Fathi et al. (2016), pp. 15ff
[166] cf. *ibid.*, 15ff
[167] cf. Christmann, *supra* note 27
[168] cf. Rabasa (2010), p. 6
[169] cf. Horgan, *supra* note 158, p. 4

the individual *"steps of deradicalization"* and biographies are so far poorly recorded. Additionally, the success of previous deradicalization programs can hardly be verified. For example, sensitive data obtained in the context of deradicalization work, which could be used to analyze (de-) radicalization processes or to evaluate the respective approaches, are generally in-project classified information and cannot be used by third parties.

The specialist literature deals mainly with the topics of radicalization and recruitment processes. Studies on deradicalization, distancing, counter-radicalization and counter-narratives are recent and sparse.[170]

In addition, the psychological and emotional factors that accompany or even favor a distancing were discussed in detail. Horgan speaks of three central factors:

The development of negative feelings as a result of membership in the extremist group (pressure, fear, the gradual elimination of fantasy and illusion); a change of priorities and a desire to rediscover what the radical scene lacks, as well as a growing disillusionment with the group's goals (e.g. failed political goals and strategies, contradictory opinions).[171]

Several studies have emphasized the need for multi-faceted approaches to deradicalization. This was also confirmed by the 2010 RAND study. A deradicalization program is particularly promising when it starts on three levels: on the affective, pragmatic and ideological levels. From this the following conclusions can be drawn: (1) the emotional connection to the radical group must be broken; (2) the practical needs of the individual, which influence the exit or stay, must be considered; and (3) an ideological debate should be made possible.[172]

There are a variety of methods that have been implemented in recent years in the context of deradicalization work. The following three approaches are presented: the systemic approach to the family, outreach work for the youth, and theological and religious offerings. Characteristics and challenges are outlined here:

---

[170] cf. Schmid, *supra* note 159
[171] cf. Horgan, *supra* note 158, pp. 4–5
[172] cf. Rabasa, *supra* note 169, p. xvi

6.2.1 Systemic consulting approaches

Systemic consulting approaches involve the social environment of the person concerned and try to have a positive effect on the person. Extremist groups, whether religious or not, often talk to their members about their human needs and desires. They try to offer solutions and interpretations on various levels. These interpretation approaches can be solidified and legitimized by the *"new given"* ideology. They cover all areas of life, starting with the social environment, social relationships (e.g. partnership, friendship, family), religious interpretation as well as interpretation and practice, values and morals, gender roles, finances, love, work, life and future planning.[173] This is the reason why it is necessary in the deradicalization to include these different levels and to edit them individually for each case. On the affective level, personal emotional reference structures and networks, the social environment and leisure time activities are strengthened. On the pragmatic level, the foundations for an autonomous life are laid and security-relevant aspects are regulated. The measures carried out here relate to the areas of security, education and prospects, work and accommodation. Through this aid, those affected will be able to emerge from their former isolation and become members of society again.[174] In dealing with the ideological level, the critical reflection of the present world view and, in the best case, a complete distancing from extremist positions should take place.

A detachment from Islam, as an individually lived religion, cannot be the goal of deradicalization work in the context of Islamism.

In the context of security and deradicalization, one often speaks of a distancing and only rarely does he deal with all pillars of deradicalization. The counseling center HAYAT-Germany[175], for example, pursues, for example, an extended approach and has the objective of also dealing with the ideological level.

In this context, dealing with narratives plays just as much a role as the critical reflection of personal attitudes and the image of the world and of man. In summary,

---

[173] cf. Fathi et al., *supra* note 166, p. 15ff

[174] cf. Dantschke (2011), online: <https://mi.sachsen-anhalt.de/fileadmin/Bibliothek/Politik_und_V erwaltung/MI/MI/4._Service/Publikationen/4._Verfassungsschutz/Brosch%C3%BCren/Tagungsband_Extremismus_Einstieg_und_Ausstieg_14122011.pd>, p. 23

[175] HAYAT is a counseling center for deradicalization, funded by the Federal Office for Migration and Refugees (<https://hayat-deutschland.de>; accessed 18 June 2018).

it can be stated that the basis for successful deradicalization work is the individual care of those directly affected and their relatives, and the targeted handling of individual problem situations.

6.2.2 Outreach youth work

Among the outreach youth work (e.g. in the form of street social work) are summarized various offers that involve the living environment of young people and reach them in public places, in youth facilities, through schools, training centers and social networks. Depending on the orientation of the projects, the adolescents will be approached through various topics and educational offers. These social space-oriented offers are partly supplemented by further fixed counseling offers. Outreach youth work by means of close-to-life speeches and low-threshold offers plays inter alia in the approaches of VAJA Bremen, IFAK e.V. with its seat in Bochum and the Violence Prevention Network an important role. This may include discussions, political education as well as recreational activities. It can be assumed that such offers tend to reach young people who have not progressed so far in their radicalization process. Additionally, the question arises as to whether pedagogical measures and offers will be sustainably accepted if there is no intrinsic motivation to cooperate with the person concerned. Outreach work and addressing the adolescents on certain topics may, under certain circumstances, also initiate discriminatory or stigmatizing processes (in the sense of a general suspicion), which in the context of a work like this must be continuously reflected by the implementing persons for the reasons stated.[176]

6.2.3 Religious offers

Religious offerings in the field of deradicalization vary widely in their implementation. The first programs with an exclusively religious approach were developed in Saudi Arabia after 9/11. These aimed specifically at the families and the social environment of the radicalized. In addition, they provided financial support for the families. These first deradicalization programs explicitly used theological experts for ideological work. In some countries, deradicalization in prisons was and is still in the hands of theological staff, with the aim of creating an ideological de-

---

[176] cf. Fathi et al., *supra* note 166, p. 15ff

tachment.[177] These first models with a theological focus cannot be one-to-one transferred to other societies.

A purely theological treatment may, inter alia, entail the danger of neglecting social, political, familial and psychological factors influencing the process of radicalization. But these are important factors that are essential for successful deradicalization work.[178] Nevertheless, it is important to offer the recipients the theological background of Islam without the extremist and violent Islamist influences.

6.2.4 Advantages and disadvantages of these approaches

At this point, I would like to state, in my opinion, every one of these approaches has advantages and disadvantages - these are weighed up against each other here briefly:

Systemic consulting approaches – advantages: Concerned persons turn to the counseling center independently (thus there is an intrinsic motivation). The advice follows an individual and biographical approach. Targeted interventions and assistance are possible. Self-initiative action activates the affected persons.

Systemic consulting approaches – disadvantages: Counseling is only at the initiative of those affected, so the coverage is considered low. Individuals who are advised, who have been "persuaded" to consult, may not be ready for the counseling process, and may therefore break it off more often than "volunteers".

Outreach youth work – advantages: A broad target group can be reached. There is direct contact with different youth milieus. It is a low-threshold offer with less access barriers.

Outreach youth work – disadvantages: There is a risk of stigmatization of adolescents. There is no intrinsic motivation in the addressed target group. It is questionable whether already radicalized young people can be reached.

Religious offers – advantages: On religious questions, can be counter-argued "authentically". To religious milieus is partially better access. The use of religious authority. The use of multipliers and "ambassadors" of Muslims.

---

[177] cf. *ibid.*, p. 15ff
[178] cf. *ibid.*, p. 15ff

Religious offers – disadvantages: The focus is on the "religiously" approachable part of the target group. The extremism problem is "theologized". The whole problem is considered as a "migration problem". The use of religious hierarchies creates new dependency structures

No matter what approach is followed, the respective action should take place under the paradigm identified by Ritzmann in 2017 – as well as the propaganda itself, the subjective credibility of the so-called mediator or transmitter of preventive and countermeasures is very important. The ability to identify with the courier essentially determines whether the content itself can be accepted.[179]

Which of the presented approaches in what contexts are successful and to what extent they can be combined, should be the subject of research in further studies. However, the fact is that all these approaches of deradicalization can benefit from the results of this master thesis - a counter strategic approach can be built up on the narratives mostly used by IS.

6.3 European level approaches

Because of the absence of evaluations of deradicalization programs in Germany, evaluations of programs of other European countries can be used to draw important conclusions about optimization possibilities and challenges that are conceivable in this area. A study by the Institute for Strategic Dialogue (ISD)[180] evaluated existing civil society programs (around right-wing extremism and Islamism). These results are of great relevance for my consideration and are presented below in part:

European approaches focus on the role of civil society and the social environment of the person concerned. Some community members can play a leading role in deradicalization work because of their knowledge and credibility as mediators between community and governmental structures. Other civil society groups can play a facilitating or supporting role by aiding and emotional or pragmatic support to those affected. Program's success often depends on the quality of the personal relationships. Trust, which is primarily based on personal rather than institutional, is particularly important. Long-term nature of a project is a decisive fac-

---

[179] cf. Ritzmann, *supra* note 51, p. 8
[180] Institute for Strategic Dialogue *supra* note 161

tor for its chances of success. Short-term financing and high turnover have had a negative impact on some projects. Competent and credible ambassadors are needed to carry out the work of deradicalization. *"Credible"* can mean a lot in this context. In Europe, these are usually people who have migration experience themselves. Imams can also be used here with in-depth religious knowledge. For some projects (such as right-wing extremism), former extremists participate as group leaders in the projects.[181]

However, experience in the UK shows that caution is needed. In 2007, the government decided to work with non-violent Salafists hoping to gain easier access to violent extremists.[182] Honestly, fundamentalist attitudes were not only tolerated by the state, but even promoted. The government of David Cameron has distanced himself from this approach and set up a four-question catalog to identify civil society cooperation partners:[183] Is the organization committed to human rights for all - including women and members of other religions? Is the organization committed to the equal rights of all people before the law? Is the organization committed to democracy and the right of the people to choose their own government? Does the organization promote integration or separatism?

These questions could also be useful in the German context. The ISD study also shows that effective state-civil society cooperation requires commitment, energy and flexibility from all partners. Lack of information and failed information exchange can affect mutual trust and damage the success of a program. This applies to civil society and security cooperation, in which both sides must be prepared to share certain information with each other. The study also indicates that a change in culture within security agencies is needed to ensure the success of civil society initiatives. Clubs and groups should be equal partners in the work of deradicalization. The challenge, however, is that a balance between civil society and state in deradicalization work is often difficult to achieve. Though, there are areas where, according to the findings of the study, no collaboration should be sought, like training religious actors or trying to reorient community structures.

Another potential challenge for state and civil society cooperation in the work of deradicalization is that communities show reservations and are reluctant to co-

---

[181] cf. Fathi et al., *supra* note 166, p. 15ff
[182] cf. Schmid, *supra* note 159
[183] *ibid.*, p. 5

operate with government officials. Marginalized communities tend to have rather bad relationships with the authorities. Their aim is to preserve their independence. Since even among radicalized people there is a fundamental skepticism towards the state, it is important that non-state actors can act without influence from the state.[184]

A particularly emphasized learning experience for planning and implementing effective deradicalization work is that the programs must be tailored to the needs of the affected community and its members. As a rule, measures of deradicalization cannot be generalized. Participation in deradicalization programs is further considered to be more effective in the ISD study if it is voluntary. Because much of the work is building relationships and strengthening the social environment is a very private process – it would not only be undesirable but ineffective, for state institutions to operate in that sphere, or for state participation to be imposed.

6.4 Excursus – "the deradicalization center of the Bavarian police"

The governmental agencies, especially the police, cannot leave the online world to extremist networks. The police – already very active in dealing with extremism offline – need to extend their activities to the online world. A combination of online and offline work, called internet referral units, is already exemplified by the Norwegian police (e.g. with online patrolling units and special Facebook police officers). The key steps in this context are notice and take action - wherein the action is not merely taking down. It also encompasses strategic analysis, communication and prevention, including anti-hate campaigns.[185] Counter, disturb and remove messages that push people in the wrong direction should be the core tasks for those agencies. At the same time, it is important to show alternatives and spread positive messages, too. But can a task like this be mastered alone by one organization?

> "It takes a network to defeat an extremist network."[186]

---

[184] cf. Fathi et al., *supra* note 166, p. 26ff

[185] cf. Lenos & Wounterse (2018), online:
<http://www.voxpol.eu/download/report/ran_pol_the_rol e-of_police_online-in_pve-and-cve_oslo_01-02_03_2018_en.pdf>, pp. 1–8

[186] *ibid.*, p. 1

Following this guiding principle, the Bavarian police started their work in September 2015 on the deradicalization of violent Islamists and Islamic extremists. For this purpose, the center for deradicalization, affiliated to the Bavarian State Office of Criminal Investigation (BLKA) was founded. A comprehensive overview of the structure and operation of the center for deradicalization is given by BT-Drs. 18/10477 from 26.06.2017, written by the current director of the institution.[187]

This competence center is part of the "Bavarian Network for Prevention and Deradicalization against Salafism", which works together with other authorities and institutions. The coordination of state measures, the content control and strategic orientation of the entire network is the task of an intra-ministerial working group (IMAG) with representatives of the interior, culture, justice and social ministry. The management of the IMAG is located at the Bavarian State Ministry of the Interior and Integration.

The Bavarian network consists of two pillars and systematically covers the two areas of *"prevention"*[188] and *"deradicalization"*. Prevention begins before a radicalization becomes apparent and addresses all social groups. Deradicalization takes place on an individual and personal basis in the case of an already recognizable radicalization. The responsibility for this pillar of *"deradicalization"* was assigned to the BLKA by the IMAG. Core tasks of this competence center are the cooperation with civil society organizations as well as a coordinating function in deradicalization cases with security relevance. Fundamental goal of the deradicalization center is to avert dangers that radically changed persons pose to others or to themselves. In cooperation with VPN, help and counseling services for the environment are formulated, such as for parents, relatives and other caregivers. At the same time distancing processes away from extremism should be triggered. In addition to analysis and assessments of context-related safety-related issues, tailored deradicalization approaches for identified radicalized persons are developed and coordinated (in the context of individual care concepts). Furthermore,

---

[187] cf. Schmidt (2017), online:
<https://www.bundestag.de/blob/511406/b87e0218049ff2687c0050f db ade5c79/18-4-922-a-data.pdf>

[188] General prevention measure (strengthening tolerance and democratic capacity, raising awareness, networking actors) and specific prevention (early detection and empowerment of specific occupational groups).

confidence-building measures in Muslim institutions are supported in an event-related context with deradicalization.

In the context of the abovementioned written statement of the BLKA in the context of a public hearing in the interior committee of the German parliament, the following statistics were published:

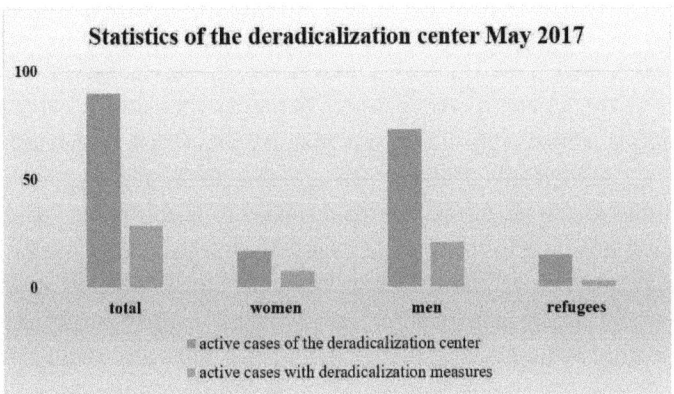

Figure 9: Statistics of the Bavarian deradicalization center

To conclude, it can be noted that the strategy used by the deradicalization center implements in practice the possible measures of deradicalization (systemic consulting approach, outreach youth work and religious offers) presented in point 6.2 in close cooperation with the civilian partner VPN and other state organizations.

6.5 Interim conclusion

The question arises, how to use the findings created from the content analysis in practice? It is important to build a bridge between science and practice – to show in which areas the mentioned results can be used, possible measures against online propaganda and possible offline measures after radicalization are introduced.

How to deal with online propaganda? One solution would be the deletion of radicalization-contents or the deactivation of IS-supporting user accounts and webpages. However, the legal basis for such measures is not entirely uncontroversial among legal scholars. Further in this context, there is the problem of encrypted communication in closed groups by Islamists. The government authorities have the problem to identify the incriminated content in the internet. Experience has shown that extremist groups behave in a conspiratorial manner in the world wide web and are usually separated from the public. On the one hand there is the problem that the radicalizing content must first be found, and on the other hand that when those are found then they are often encrypted. Overall, it can be stated that measures such as deliberate deletion of accounts and content or the decryption of messages are controversial discussed in terms of their impact and legality.

The second solution against the effects of online propaganda, is the use of so-called *"counter-narratives"*. At its core, this means exposing incongruities and contradictions in the Islamic narratives and offering an alternative view of things. This *"counter-narratives"* should use rational and emotional arguments. A balanced mix of proactive and defensive narratives should be applied. Ideally, these interpretations are disseminated by ex-IS members or people around them. State actors should step back in the spread of these narratives in order not to cause a fundamental rejection of the recipient. Therefore, joint ventures with NGOs should be versed. But the theory of *"counter-narrative"* is controversial discussed, too. Honestly, there are no currently reliable studies about the causal success of counter narrative measures. The issue of appropriate countermeasures against Islamist online propaganda is a major challenge for governments, civil society and science alike.

What measures can be taken offline to prevent radicalization or to deradicalize? First of all, it has to be stated that radicalization has to be understood as a process. As a process, that is determined by many different factors, that there are many paths into radical scenes and that the influencing factors of this process can be very different. Exactly for this reason deradicalization measures should be understand as a process, that must be tailored different to each person and every approach and program must be individualized. Three of the most promising approaches are *"systemic consulting approaches"*, *"outreach youth work"* and *"religious offers"*.

"Systemic consulting approaches" involve the social environment of the person concerned and try to have a positive effect on the person. Personal emotional reference structures and networks, the social environment and leisure time activities are strengthened. These structures can be strengthened and developed through state-controlled measures in the areas of security, education and perspectives, work and housing. With this aid affected can emerge from their former isolation and become members of society again - with no Islamist worldview. Among *"Outreach youth work"* are summarized various offers that involve the liv-

ing environment of young people and reach them in those places they usually spend their time. Though, it must be assumed that such offers reach young people who have not progressed so far in their radicalization process. *"Religious offers"* in the field of deradicalization vary widely in their implementation. It is important to offer the recipients the theological background of Islam without the extremist and violent Islamist influences.

Each of these three approaches has got its advantages and disadvantages. I am firmly convinced that a good mix of these approaches in the sense of concerted actions is not only the most promising but can also (in times of scarce resources) create positive synergy effects.

European level approaches were evaluated by a study of the ISD. Here was stated, that European level focuses the role of civil society and the social environment. The success of deradicalization programs depends on the quality of the personal relationships between all role players. Trust, which is primarily based on personal rather than institutional, is particularly important. Projects must be long-termed to have prospects of success. Short-term financing and high turnover had a negative impact on deradicalization projects. Competent and credible ambassadors are needed to carry out the deradicalization work (like Imams or people with migration experience themselves). In this context, it is important to know who works for the civilian partner organizations - that accidentally Salafist or violent scenes will not be promoted with state support. As a rule, measures of deradicalization cannot be generalized. Participation in deradicalization programs is further considered to be more effective in the ISD study if it is voluntary. Because much of the work is building relationships and strengthening the social environment is a very private process - it would not only be undesirable but ineffective, for state institutions to operate in that sphere, or for state participation to be imposed.

On Bavaria level was the deradicalization center of the Bavarian police founded in 2015 – for online and offline fight against radicalization. It is assigned to the BLKA. Its core tasks are the cooperation with civil society organizations as well as coordinating function in deradicalization cases with security relevance. On Bavarian level the partner of the state security agencies is the NGO VPN. The focus of work is in analyzing and assessing the context-related safety related issues, developing and coordinating tailored deradicalization approaches for identified radicalized persons. Furthermore, confidence-building measures in Muslim institutions are supported in deradicalization context. The strategy used by the deradicalization center implements in practice the above-mentioned measures.

7 Conclusion and suggestions for further research

7.1 Conclusion

Based on my research interest in combating Islamic terrorism in the West more successfully, in particular through effective work in the field of deradicalization, the flagship of IS propaganda – IS one of the most dangerous terrorist organizations worldwide – was analyzed with the following question: *What are contents of English-language propaganda published form the Islamic State in the online magazine "Rumiyah", which offer a radicalization potential for Western recipients?* For this purpose, a category system derived from radicalization research was applied to the analysis material. Subsequently, the results were compared with an evaluation of the precursor, the *"Dabiq"* magazine, from the secondary literature. Finally, possible approaches for constructive deradicalization work were presented, which can be made more effective by using the results of my analysis work.

One of the most important observations is, that IS propaganda takes up all typically motives of radicalization. This suggests that the well-known mechanisms of combating radicalization are equally applicable to IS's ones. However, special attention should be paid to the mainstream of propaganda in these actions. My analysis shows that the main focus is on the construction of a simplified "good-evil" or "friend-enemy" dichotomy in connection with a glorifying self-portrayal of IS's own achievements and heroes. IS derives its legitimacy and credibility in its propaganda about its claim to sole representation of Islam, which is based on its own interpretation of the Quran. The analysis clearly showed that, in the context of the above-mentioned formation of the simplified differentiated view of the world, emphasis is placed on delimiting the teachings of the IS from other faiths of Islam. These demarcations are always related to IS's self-expression as a superior elitist society of Allah's chosen ones.

These findings from the analysis of the texts of the *"Rumiyah"* magazine are underpinned by the used layout. From issue to issue, this was made more professionally and is intended, through the language of the images, to reinforce precisely the radicalization motifs mentioned. In addition, life in the IS is depicted as – normal life with regular everyday life. Terrifying is the presentation of detailed instructions for the conduct of lone wolf attacks as well as the provision of radicalizing content for PC and mobile devices tailored for children – the youngest possible recipients.

Comparing with the analysis results of the "*Dabiq*" magazine from the secondary literature, it can be stated that the direction of the propaganda changed in two points: There is an offensive advertisement for the jihad in the Western countries (no more for the *hijra* to IS) and the detailed differentiated concept of the enemy gives way to a more global "good-evil" concept. In the layout, the key point is that the "*Ruminyah*" is easier for recipients to read (simpler written) and has less theological (too theoretical) content.

These identified priorities and the IS-specific design of the radicalization motifs can be incorporated into the online and offline measures of the government agencies for deradicalization. In the area of "counter-narratives", the simplified and differentiated world view has to be shaken up by means of rational and emotional arguments. Facts underpinned by well-founded religious content and a presentation of reality in terms of life in IS's occupied territories are an effective means of doing so. In dealing with already radicalized recipients or in prevention work, a good mix of the various presented approaches are expedient. To bring the peaceful religion of Islam closer to potential recipients of radicalized content and to integrate them into their social environment must be the aimed goal. These deradicalization measures should be long-termed, mediated by credible ambassadors (hand in hand working state security agencies closely with NGOs)

Only a simultaneous fight against radicalization in society with accompanying deradicalization measures and targeted counter-propaganda on a virtual level can lead to a lasting containment of Islamist terrorism and increase international security in the long term.

7.2 Suggestions for further research

Further studies should investigate which distribution channels the media wing of the IS uses to disseminate his contents (especially which internet platforms are used with which target direction). This is particularly important for research, because as a matter of fact the magazine "*Rumiyah*" no longer appears since September 2017 - and the question arises, which kind of media is used by IS now to disseminate its radical ideas to recipients.

More than language, the impact of pictures on the radicalization process can be seen. An analysis of the pictures used and their psychological impact on the inclined reader would be further enlightening, in conjunction with a content analysis, and would provide new starting points for building up tailored counternarratives.

In the light of the current political situation in Europe, in the context of the "large wave of refugees to Europe", the question also arises as to whether and to what extent the IS deliberately seeks to radicalize migrants. As described in this master thesis, it is one of IS's stated goals to carry *jihad* to the Western countries. Researching these radicalization methods and pathways would be necessary in order to prevent (relating thereto) lone wolf terrorism at an early stage and to initiate the required countermeasures just in time on the part of the state security organizations.

8 References

8.1 Analysis material

N.N. (2016a) "Rumiyah (issue 1)," https://jihadology.net/category/rome-magazine/ (accessed 12 June 2018).

N.N. (2016b) "Rumiyah (issue 2)," https://jihadology.net/category/rome-magazine/ (accessed 12 June 2018).

N.N. (2016c) "Rumiyah (issue 3)," https://jihadology.net/category/rome-magazine/ (accessed 12 June 2018).

N.N. (2016d) "Rumiyah (issue 4)," https://jihadology.net/category/rome-magazine/ (accessed 12 June 2018).

N.N. (2017a) "Rumiyah (issue 10): The Jihad in East Asia," https://jihadology.net/category/rome-magazine/ (accessed 12 June 2018).

N.N. (2017b) "Rumiyah (issue 11): The ruling on ghanimah, fay, and ihtitab," https://jihadology.net/category/rome-magazine/ (accessed 12 June 2018).

N.N. (2017c) "Rumiyah (issue 12): It will be a fire that burns; the cross and its people in Raqqah," https://jihadology.net/category/rome-magazine/ (accessed 12 June 2018).

N.N. (2017d) "Rumiyah (issue 13): Allah cast Terror into their hearts," https://jihadology.net/category/rome-magazine/ (accessed 12 June 2018).

N.N. (2017e) "Rumiyah (issue 5)," https://jihadology.net/category/rome-magazine/ (accessed 12 June 2018).

N.N. (2017f) "Rumiyah (issue 6)," https://jihadology.net/category/rome-magazine/ (accessed 12 June 2018).

N.N. (2017g) "Rumiyah (issue 7): Establishing the Islamic State; between the prophetic methodology and the Paths of the deviants," https://jihadology.net/category/rome-magazine/ (accessed 12 June 2018).

N.N. (2017h) "Rumiyah (issue 8): Among the believers are men; Shaykh Abu Sulayman Ash-Shami," https://jihadology.net/category/rome-magazine/ (accessed 12 June 2018).

N.N. (2017i) "Rumiyah (issue 9): The ruling on the belligerent Christians," https://jihadology.net/category/rome-magazine/ (accessed 12 June 2018).

8.2 Literature

Al-Ibrahim, Bader (2015) "ISIS, Wahhabism and Takfir." 8 Contemporary Arab Affairs. 408-415.

Al-Saud, Abdullah bbin Khaled (2017) "The Tranquillity Campaign: A Beacon of Light in the Dark World Wide Web." 11 Perspectives on Terrorism. 58-64.

Awan, Akil (2016) "Virtual jihadist media." 10 European Journal of Cultural Studies. 389-408.

Böckler, Nils & Zick, Andreas (2015) "Im Sog des Pop-Dschihadismus." 2015 DJI impulse. 18-22.

Braddock, Kurt & Horgan, John (2015) "Towards a Guide for Constructing and Disseminating Counternarratives to Reduce Support for Terrorism." 39 Studies in Conflict & Terrorism. 381-404.

Brasher, Brenda (2004) Give me that online religion, New Brunswick, N.J: Rutgers University Press.

Briggs, Rachel, Fieschi, Catherine & Lownsbrough, Hannah (2006) Bringing it home: Community-based approaches to counter-terrorism, London: Demos.

Buchta, Wilfried (2015) Terror vor Europas Toren: Der Islamische Staat, Iraks Zerfall und Amerikas Ohnmacht, Frankfurt am Main: Campus Verlag.

Bussemer, Thymian (2005) Propaganda: Konzepte und Theorien, Wiesbaden, s.l.: VS Verlag für Sozialwissenschaften.

Cesari, Jocelyne & Pisoiu, Daniela (2015) "Radicalization," in J. Cesari, ed., The Oxford handbook of European Islam, Oxford, New York, NY: Oxford University Press, 10-42.

Colas, Brandon (2016) "What Does Dabiq Do?: ISIS Hermeneutics and Organizational Fractures within Dabiq Magazine." 40 Studies in Conflict & Terrorism. 173-190.

Commins, David Dean (2006) The Wahhabi mission and Saudi Arabia, London, New York: I.B. Tauris.

Delanty, Gerard & Kumar, Krishan (2006) The SAGE handbook of nations and nationalism, London, Thousand Oaks, Calif.: SAGE.

Farwell, James P. (2014) "The Media Strategy of ISIS." 56 Survival. 49-55.

Fathi, Alma, Mansour, Ahmad, Müller, Jochen, Waleciak Julian, Nordbruch, Götz & el Mafaalani, Aladin (2016) Ansätze und Erfahrungen der Präventions- und Deradikalisierungsarbeit, Frankfurt/Main: HSFK.

Friis, Simone Mollin (2015) "'Beyond anything we have ever seen': Beheading videos and the visibility of violence in the war against ISIS." 91 International Affairs. 725-746.

Gambhir, Harleen (2016) The Virtual Caliphate: ISIS's Information Warfare, Washington D.C.

Ghaussy, Ghanie (1989) "Der islamistische Fundamentalismus der Gegenwart," in T. Meyer, ed., Fundamentalismus in der modernen Welt: Die Internationale der Unvernunft, Frankfurt a.M.: Suhrkamp, 83-100.

Glaser, Michaela (2007) "Gewaltorientierter Islamismus im Jugendalter. Eine Diskussion vorliegender Erkenntnisse zu Hinwendungsmotiven und Attraktivitätsmomenten für junge Menschen." Kinder- und Jugendschutz in Wissenschaft und Praxis: Islamischer Radikalisierung Jugendlicher vorbeugen. 3-7.

Glazzard, Andrew (2017) "Losing the Plot: Narrative, Counter-Narrative and Violent Extremism." Terrorism and Counter-Terrorism Studies.

Hall, Benjamin (2015) Inside ISIS: The brutal rise of a terrorist army, New York: Center Street.

Horgan, John (2010) "Deradicalization or Disengagement?" 2 Perspectives on Terrorism.

Hughes, Seamus, & Alexander Meleagrou-Hitchens (2017) "The Threat to the United States from the Islamic State's Virtual Entrepreneurs." 10 CTC Senitnel. 1-8.

Ingram, Haroro (2016) "An analysis of Islamic State's Dabiq magazine." 51 Australian Journal of Political Science. 458-477.

Krämer, Gudrun (2002) "Islam ist nicht gleich Islam - Einheit der Lehre, Vielfalt der Lebenswelten," in W. Weiss, ed., Handbuch Islam, Köln: DuMont-Monte-Verl., 18-25.

Lahoud, Nelly, Miltion, Daniel, Price, Bryan & al-'Ubaydi, Muhammad (2014) The Group That Calls Itself a State: Understanding the Evolution and Challenges of the Islamic State, Fort Belvoir, VA: Defense Technical Information Center.

Lakomy, Miron (2017) "Cracks in the Online "Caliphate": How the Islamic State is Losing Ground in the Battle for Cyberspace." 11 Perspectives on Terrorism.

Leggewie, Claus (2002) Auf dem Weg zum Euro-Islam?: Moscheen und Muslime in der Bundesrepublik Deutschland ; Vortrag anläßlich der Vorstellung des Handbuchs „Der Weg zur Moschee - eine Handreichung für die Praxis" in der Hessischen Landesvertretung, Berlin, am 14. Mai 2002, Bad Homburg v.d. Höhe: Herbert-Quandt-Stiftung.

Liberman, Ariel Victoria (2017) "Terrorism, the Internet, and Propaganda: A Deadly Combination." 9 Journal of NAtional Security Law & Policy. 95-124.

Liebl, Vernie (2009) "The Caliphate." 45 Middle Eastern Studies. 373-391.

Marty, Martin & Appleby, Scott (1994) Fundamentalisms observed, Chicago.

Mayer, Tilman (2006) "Zeichen des Krieges - Krieg der Zeichen: Die islamistische Provokation," in M. Meyer-Blanck & G. K. Hasselhoff, eds., Krieg der Zeichen?: Zur Interaktion von Religion, Politik und Kultur, Würzburg: Ergon-Verl., 181-88.

Mayring, Philipp (2010) Qualitative Inhaltsanalyse: Grundlagen und Techniken, Weinheim u.a.: Beltz.

McCants, William F. (2015) The ISIS apocalypse: The history, strategy, and doomsday vision of the Islamic State, New York: Picador; St. Martin's Press.

McCauley, Clark & Moskalenko, Sophia (2008) "Mechanisms of Political Radicalization: Pathways Toward Terrorism." 20 Terrorism and Political Violence. 415-433.

Moghaddam, Fathali (2005) "The staircase to terrorism: A psychological exploration." 60 The American psychologist. 161-169.

Mohomed, Carimo (2014) ""Islam" as the national identity for the formation of Pakistan: The political thought of Muhammad Iqbal and Abu'l 'Ala Mawdudi." 33 História (São Paulo). 217-339.

Neumann, Peter (2013) "Radikalisierung, Deradikalisierung und Extremismus." 63. Aus Politik und Zeitgeschichte: Deradikalisierung. 3-10.

Neumann, Peter (2015) Die neuen Dschihadisten: ISIS, Europa und die nächste Welle des Terrorismus, Berlin: Ullstein eBooks.

Nitsch, Holger (2001) Terrorismus und internationale Politik am Ende des 20. Jahrhunderts: Vergleichende Studie über Gemeinsamkeiten und Unterschiede verschiedener Ansätze und Definitionen von Terrorismus - insbesondere in seiner internationalen Ausprägung - und extremistischer Organisationen in Struktur, Entwicklung und Arbeitsweise anhand ausgewählter Beispiele und Vereinigungen, mit dem Ziel einer Typologie des Phänomens. München, Unv., Diss., 2001, München.

Ohlig, Karl-Heinz & Stölting, Ulrike Stölting (2000) Weltreligion Islam: Eine Einführung, Mainz, Luzern: Matthias-Grünewald-Verl.; Ed. Exodus.

Peresin, Anita & Cervone, Alberto (2015) "The Western Muhajirat of ISIS." 38 Studies in Conflict & Terrorism. 495-509.

Pohjonen, Matti & Ahmed, Reem (2016) "Narratives of Risk: Assessing the Discourse of Online Extremism and Measures Proposed to Counter It." 34 Sicherheit & Frieden. 236-241.

Prucha, Nico (2015) "Kriegsführung 2.0." DJI Impulse: Jung und Radikal. Politische Gewalt im Jugendalter. 22-25.

Qadir, Hanif (2016) Preventing and countering extremism and terrorism recruitment: A best practice guide, Catt Educational.

Rabasa, Angel (2010) Deradicalizing Islamist extremists, Santa Monica, Calif.: RAND.

Rabasa, Angel & Bernard, Cheryl (2015) Eurojihad: Patterns of Islamist radicalization and terrorism in Europe, Cambridge: Cambridge University Press.

Rauf, Ceylan, & Jokisch, Benjamin, eds. (2014) Salafismus in Deutschland: Entstehung, Radikalisierung und Prävention, Frankfurt, M.: Lang-Ed.

Ritzmann, Alexander (2017) "Propaganda: Wirkung, Grenzen und Gegenmaß-nahmen." 9 Interventionen. Zeitschrift für Veranwortungspädagogik. 4-9.

Snow, David & Scott, Byrd (2007) "Ideology, Framing Processes, and Islamic Terrorist Movements." 12 Mobilization. 119-136.

Stern, Jessica & Berger, John (2015) ISIS: The state of terror, New York, N.Y: Ecco Press, an imprint of HarperCollinsPublishers.

Taken, Jens & Kevenhörster, Paul (2012) "Radikalisierung und Deradikalisierung im transnationalen islamistischen Terrorismus," Dissertation.

Wainwright, Rob (2017) European Union Terrorism situation and trend report (te-sat) 2017, Den Haag.

Weimann, Gabriel (2015) Terrorism in Cyberspace: The Next Generation, New York: Columbia University Press.

Weiss, Michael, & Hassan Hassan (2015) ISIS: Inside the army of terror, New York, NY: Regan Arts.

Wiktorowicz, Quintan (2005) Radical Islam Rising: Muslim Extremism in the West, Lanham: Rowman & Littlefield Publishers.

Zelin, Aron (2015) "Picture Or It Didn't Happen: A Snapshot of the Islamic State's Official Media Output." 9 Perspectives on Terrorism. 85-97.

8.3 Online sources

Al-Tamimi, Aymenn, Jawad (2014) "The Dawn of the Islamic State of Iraq and ash-Sham," http://www.aymennjawad.org/14363/the-dawn-of-the-islamic-state-of-iraq-and-ash-sham (accessed 29 May 2018).

Atwan, Abdel, Bari (2015) "A Portrait of Caliph Ibrahim," https://www.thecairoreview.com/essays/a-portrait-of-caliph-ibrahim/ (accessed 19 June 2018).

Barrett, Richard (2015) "Foreign Fighters: An Updated Assessment of the Flow of Foreign Fighters into Syria and Iraq," http://soufangroup.com/wp-content/uploads/2015/12/TSG_ForeignFightersUpdate3.pdf (accessed 29 May 2018).

BayLV (Landesamt für Verfassungsschutz Bayern) (2017) "Verfassungsschutz-bericht Bayern 2016,"
http://www.verfassungsschutz.bayern.de/ueberuns/medien/publikation en/index.html (accessed 22 August 2017).

BfV (Bundesamt für Verfassungsschutz) (2017) "Verfassungsschutzbericht 2016,"
https://www.verfassungsschutz.de/de/oeffentlichkeitsarbeit/publikation en/verfassungsschutzberichte (accessed 22 August 2017).

BfV (Bundesamt für Verfassungsschutz) (2018) "Kommunikationsstrategie des IS,"
https://www.verfassungsschutz.de/de/aktuelles/schlaglicht/schlaglicht-2016-12-kommunikationsstrategie-des-is (accessed 15 June 2018).

BfV (Bundesamt für Verfassungsschutz) (2018) "Verfassungsschutzbericht 2017,"
https://www.verfassungsschutz.de/de/oeffentlichkeitsarbeit/publikation en/verfassungsschutzberichte (accessed 16 June 2018).

Bin Laden, Osama (2002) "Letter to Mullah Muhammed 'Umar from Bin Laden – Combating Terrorism Center at West Point,"
https://ctc.usma.edu/harmony-program/letter-to-mullah-muhammed-umar-from-bin-laden-original-language-2/ (accessed 15 June 2018).

BKA (Bundeskriminalamt) (2018) "PKS 2017,"
https://www.bka.de/DE/AktuelleInformationen/StatistikenLagebilder/P olizeilicheKriminalstatistik/PKS2016/pks2016_node.html (accessed 16 June 2018).

Christmann, Kris (2012) "Preventing Religious Radicalisation and Violent Ex-tremism: A Systematic Review of the Research Evidence,"
https://pure.hud.ac.uk/en/publications/preventing-religious-radicalisation-and-violent-extremism-a-syste (accessed 11 June 2018).

Comerford, Milo (2016) "What Isis lost in Dabiq,"
https://www.newstatesman.com/politics/staggers/2016/10/what-isis-lost-dabiq (accessed 16 June 2018).

Dantschke, Claudia (2011) "Ausstieg aus dem islamistischen Extremismus: Vortrag bei „Extremismus - Einstieg und Austieg", Fachtagung zur Neuausrichtung von Ausstiegshilfen,," https://mi.sachsen-an-halt.de/fileadmin/Bibliothek/Politik_und_Verwaltung/MI/MI/4._Service/Publikatio-nen/4._Verfassungsschutz/Brosch%C3%BCren/Tagungsband_Extremismus_Einstieg_und_Ausstieg_14122011.pd (accessed 17 June 2018).

Dehn, Ulrich (2006) "Islam im Kontext der Fundamentalismusdebatte," http://www.ezw-berlin.de/html/15_1129.php (accessed 24 May 2018).

Deutscher Bundestag (2017) "Drucksache 18/11970 vom 07.04.2017," https://www.bundestag.de/blob/503858/029b5f6683ed2807959d7e1c55853af0/antisemtismusbericht_bericht-data.pdf (accessed 26 September 2017).

Dodd, Vikram (2016) "Police study links radicalisation to mental health problems," https://www.theguardian.com/uk-news/2016/may/20/police-study-radicalisation-mental-health-problems (accessed 16 June 2018).

Friedland, Elliot (2016) "Latest Issue of ISIS Rumiyah Magazine Released," https://clarionproject.org/latest-issue-isis-rumiyah-magazine-released/ (accessed 17 July 2018).

Hegghammer, Thomas (2013) "Should I Stay or Should I Go? Explaining Variation in Western Jihadists' Choice between Domestic and Foreign Fighting," http://www.start.umd.edu/news/hegghammer-explains-variation-western-jihadists (accessed 12 June 2018).

Hegghammer, Thomas & Nesser, Petter (2015) "Assessing the Islamic State's Commitment to Attacking the West," http://www.terrorismanalysts.com/pt/index.php/pot/article/view/440/html (accessed 29 May 2018).

Holman, Timothy (2015) "The Swarm: Terrorist Incidents in France," https://jamestown.org/program/the-swarm-terrorist-incidents-in-france/ (accessed 12 June 2018).

Hughes, Seamus & Vidino, Lorenzo (2015) "ISIS in America: From Retweets to Raqqa: Program on Extremism," https://cchs.gwu.edu/panel-discussion-isis-america-retweets-raqqa (accessed 21 August 2017).

Ingram, Haroro & Reed, Alastair (2017) "Exploring the Role of Instructional Material in AQAP's Inspire and ISIS' Rumiyah," https://icct.nl/wp-content/uploads/2017/06/reeda_ingramh_instructionalmaterial.pdf (accessed 12 June 2018).

Institute for Strategic Dialogue (2010) "The role of civil society in counter-radicalisation and de-radicalisation: PPN-working paper," http://bit.ly/24B5ceX (accessed 17 June 2018).

Joscelyn, Thomas (2016) "Town of Dabiq falls to Turkish-backed forces | FDD's Long War Journal," https://www.longwarjournal.org/archives/2016/10/town-of-dabiq-falls-to-turkish-backed-forces.php (accessed 29 May 2018).

Kasper, Amy (2017) "Counter-Narratives and the 'Backfire Effect'," http://www.leidensafetyandsecurityblog.nl/articles/counter-narratives-and-the-backfire-effect (accessed 13 June 2018).

Kaye, David (2017) "Mandate of the Special Rapporteur on the promotion and protection of the right to freedom of opinion and expression," https://www.ohchr.org/Documents/Issues/Opinion/Legislation/OL-DEU-1-2017.pdf (accessed 12 June 2018).

Kiefer, Maximilian, Messing, Kira, Musial, Julia & Weiß, Tobias (2017) "Westliche Jugendliche im Bann des Islamischen Staates - Radikalisierende Inhalte der IS-Propaganda am Beispiel der Onlinemagazine Dabiq und Rumiyah," http://journals.sfu.ca/jd/index.php/jd/article/view/75 (accessed 21 August 2017).

Lenos, Steven & Wounterse, Lieke (2018) "The role of police online in PVE and CVE: It takes a network to defeat an extremist network," http://www.voxpol.eu/download/report/ran_pol_the_role-of_police_online-in_pve-and-cve_oslo_01-02_03_2018_en.pdf (accessed 15 June 2018).

Lipka, Michael & Hackett, Conrad (2017) "Why Muslims are the world's fastest-growing religious group?," http://www.pewresearch.org/fact-tank/2017/04/06/why-muslims-are-the-worlds-fastest-growing-religious-group/ (accessed 24 May 2018).

Maaßen, Hans-Georg (2014) "Themenschwerpunkte „jihadistischer" Propaganda im Internet,"
https://www.verfassungsschutz.de/de/oeffentlichkeitsarbeit/p ublikationen/pb-islamismus/faltblatt-2014-07-themenschwerpunkte-jihadistischer-propaganda (accessed 21 August 2017).

McKernan, Bethan (2016) "Isis' new magazine Rumiyah shows the terror group is 'struggling to adjust to losses',"
http://www.independent.co.uk/news/world/middle-east/isis-propaganda-terror-group-losses-syria-iraq-a7228286.html (accessed 26 September 2017).

McDowell-Smith, Allison, Speckhard, Anne & Yayla, Ahmet (2017) "Beating ISIS in the Digital Space: Focus Testing ISIS Defector Counter-Narrative Videos with American College Students,"
http://journals.sfu.ca/jd/index.php/jd/article/view/83 (accessed 13 June 2018).

McFarlane, Bruce (2011) "Online Violent Radicalisation (OVeR): Challenges facing Law Enforcement Agencies and Policy Stakeholders,"
http://1dneox4dyqrx1207m11b46y7tfi.wpengine.netdna-cdn.com/radicalisation/files/2013/03/ (accessed 13 July 2018).

McKernan, Bethan (2016) "The new Isis magazine is hiding a huge signal the group's days may be numbered,"
https://www.independent.co.uk/news/world/middle-east/isis-propaganda-terror-group-losses-syria-iraq-a7228286.html (accessed 16 June 2018).

N.N. "Statistik der Religionen in Deutschland," https://www.remid.de/archiv-mit-dokumentationsstelle/ (accessed 24 May 2018).

N.N. (2014) "Islamic State's (ISIS, ISIL) Horrific Magazine,"
https://clarionproject.org/islamic-state-isis-isil-propaganda-magazine-dabiq-50/ (accessed 29 May 2018).

N.N. (2015) "Islamic State's Caliphate Shrinks by 14 Percent in 2015: 12,800 km2 lost, now controls 78,000 km2 in Iraq and Syria; Syrian Kurds expand territory by 186 percent," http://news.ihsmarkit.com/press-release/aerospace-defense-security/islamic-states-caliphate-shrinks-14-percent-2015 (accessed 29 May 2018).

N.N. (2016a) "Rumiyah (issue 1)," https://jihadology.net/category/rome-magazine/ (accessed 12 June 2018).

N.N. (2016b) "Rumiyah (issue 2)," https://jihadology.net/category/rome-magazine/ (accessed 12 June 2018).

N.N. (2016c) "Rumiyah (issue 3)," https://jihadology.net/category/rome-magazine/ (accessed 12 June 2018).

N.N. (2016d) "Rumiyah (issue 4)," https://jihadology.net/category/rome-magazine/ (accessed 12 June 2018).

N.N. (2017) "Chronologie: Attacken auf Europas Metropolen," http://www.spiegel.de/politik/ausland/terrorismus-in-europa-eine-chronologie-a-1150645.html (accessed 18 July 2018).

N.N. (2017a) "Rumiyah (issue 10): The Jihad in East Asia," https://jihadology.net/category/rome-magazine/ (accessed 12 June 2018).

N.N. (2017b) "Rumiyah (issue 5)," https://jihadology.net/category/rome-magazine/ (accessed 12 June 2018).

N.N. (2017c) "Rumiyah (issue 9): The ruling on the belligerent Christians," https://jihadology.net/category/rome-magazine/ (accessed 12 June 2018).

Neumann, Peter (2015) "Insight Paper Report Back Foreign fighter total in Syria/Iraq now exceeds 20,000: surpasses Afghanistan conflict in the 1980s," http://icsr.info/2015/01/foreign-fighter-total-syriairaq-now-exceeds-20000-surpasses-afghanistan-conflict-1980s/ (accessed 29 May 2018).

Paulussen, Christophe, Nijman, Janne & Lismont, Karlien (2017) "Mental Health and the Foreign Fighter Phenomenon: A Case Study from the Netherlands," https://icct.nl/wp-content/uploads/2017/03/ICCT-Paulussen-Nijman-Lismont-Mental-Health-and-the-Foreign-Fighter-Phenomenon-March-2017-1.pdf (accessed 16 June 2018).

Pragalath, Kuang (2016) "Rumiyah would not replace Dabiq," https://www.beritadaily.com/rumiyah-would-not-replace-dabiq/ (accessed 17 July 2018).

Rossi, Sabine (2016) ""Amaq" - das Sprachrohr der Terroristen,"
http://www.tagesschau.de/amaq-nachrichtenagentur-101.html (accessed
15 June 2018).

Roy, Oliver (2015) "What is the driving force behind jihadist terrorism? - A scientific perspective on the causes/circumstances of joining the scene: Kon-
ferenzpapier der Herbstkonferenz des Bundeskriminalamts: International
Terrorism: How can prevention keep peace?,"
https://www.bka.de/SharedDocs/Downloads/EN/Publications/AutumnC
onferences/2015/herbsttagung2015RoyAbstract.html (accessed 21 August 2017).

Ryan, Michael (2014) "Hot Issue: Dabiq: What Islamic State's New Magazine
Tells Us about Their Strategic Direction, Recruitment Patterns and Guer-
rilla Doctrine," https://jamestown.org/program/hot-issue-dabiq-what-
islamic-states-new-magazine-tells-us-about-their-strategic-direction-
recruitment-patterns-and-guerrilla-doctrine/ (accessed 29 May 2018).

Saltman, Erin Marie & Smith, Melanie (2015) "Till Martyrdom Do US Part: Gender and the ISIS Phenomenon," https://www.isdglobal.org/wp-
con-
tent/uploads/2016/02/Till_Martyrdom_Do_Us_Part_Gender_and_the_ISIS
_Phenomenon.pdf (accessed 12 June 2018).

Schmid, Alex (2013) "Radicalisation, De-Radicalisation, Counter-Radicalisation:
A Conceptual Discussion and Literature Review,"
https://www.icct.nl/download/file/ICCT-Schmid-Radicalisation-De-
Radicalisation-Counter-Radicalisation-March-2013_2.pdf (accessed 17
June 2018).

Schmidt, Holger (2017) "Beitrag zur öffentlichen Anhörung des Innenaus-
schusses des Deutschen Bundestages: Drs. 18/10477 - eine bundesweite
Präventionsstrategie gegen den gewaltbereiten Islamismus,"
https://www.bundestag.de/blob/511406/b87e0218049ff2687c0050fdb
ade5c79/18-4-922-a-data.pdf (accessed 19 June 2018).

Schubert, Martina (2015) "Brutal und schnell: Die Medienstrategie des IS,"
https://www.pro-
medienmagazin.de/gesellschaft/weltweit/2015/11/23/brutal-und-
schnell-die-medienstrategie-des-is/ (accessed 15 June 2018).

Simpson, John & Weiner, Edmund (2017) "Oxford Dictionaries: Definition 'lone wolf," https://en.oxforddictionaries.com/definition/lone_wolf (accessed 18 July 2018).

Spada, Andrea (2016) "Rumiyah, the new Islamic State magazine glosses over reality of caliphate," http://www.islamedianalysis.info/rumiyah-the-new-islamic-state-magazine-glosses-over-reality-of-caliphate/ (accessed 17 July 2018).

Spencer, Richard & Connor, Neil (2015) "Number of foreign fighters in Iraq and Syria 'has doubled in past year' - Telegraph," http://www.telegraph.co.uk/news/worldnews/islamic-state/12038402/Number-of-foreign-fighters-in-Iraq-and-Syria-has-doubled-in-past-year.html (accessed 21 August 2017).

Spindler, Gerald (2017) "Gutachten zum Netzwerkdurchsetzunsgesetz," https://www.bitkom.org/Bitkom/Publikationen/Gutachten-von-Prof-Dr-Gerald-Spindler-zum-Netzwerkdurchsetzunsgesetz.html (accessed 12 June 2018).

Veilleux-Lapage, Yannik (2014) "Retweeting the Caliphate: The Role of Soft-Sympathizers in the Islamic State's Social Media Strategy," https://www.academia.edu/9809988/_Retweeting_the_Caliphate_The_Role_of_Soft_Sympathizers_in_the_Islamic_State_s_Social_Media_Strategy_Paper_presented_at_the_6th_International_Symposium_on_Terrorism_and_Transnational_Crime_in_Antalya_Turkey (accessed 13 July 2018).

Winter, Charlie (2014) "Media Jihad: The Islamic State's Doctrine for Information Warfare," http://icsr.info/2017/02/icsr-report-media-jihad-islamic-states-doctrine-information-warfare/ (accessed 14 June 2018).

Wood, Graeme (2015) "What ISIS Really Wants," https://www.theatlantic.com/magazine/archive/2015/03/what-isis-really-wants/384980/ (accessed 29 May 2018).

Young, Holly, Zwenk, Frederike & Rooze, Magda (2013) "TerRA (Terrorism and Radicalisation) - A review of the literature on radicalisation; and what it means for TerRa," http://www.terra-net.eu/files/publications/20140227160036Literature%20review%20incl%20cover%20in%20color.pdf (accessed 11 June 2018).

Zeit online (2014) "Extremismus : Zahl gewaltbereiter Islamisten steigt stark an," http://www.zeit.de/politik/2014-06/Polizeigewerkschaft-Islamisten (accessed 21 August 2017).

Zelin, Aron (2018) "al-Ḥayāt Media Center," https://jihadology.net/category/al-%E1%B8%A5ayat-media-center/ (accessed 15 June 2018).

9 Appendix

9.1 Definitions

9.1.1 Muslim vs. Islamist

Around 1.8 billion people profess their faith in Islam,[189] one of the world's major religions, i.e. about 24 percent of the total world population. This makes Islam the second largest religious community in the world after Christianity.

The Islamic societies can – simplified – be assigned to three cultural characteristics: We are talking about Arab Islam with about 180 million people, the so-called Indo-Islam, which includes Pakistan, Bangladesh, Indonesia and India itself, and finally the so-called Afro-Islam in sub-Saharan Africa.[190] The immigration of work seeking people into the industrialized countries of the First World has made Islam a strong minority religion in Europe and in North America over the past decades. Today round about 3.3 million Muslims live in Germany.[191] For the immigrant Muslims, the concept of Euro-Islam has emerged and is discussed in scientific literature.[192] However, the Muslims of the world live not only in different cultural contexts but also in very different political systems, which are partly against ideals of unity and the variety of sources of beliefs.[193] The Koran, the central religious script, and the Sunna, the tradition of the Prophet, are not only complex, meaningful and not free of contradictions, but are also differently interpreted by different religious schools and religious directions. There is no institution in Islam with central interpretive authority, instead a great variety of interpretations. There is a great willingness in the Muslim world to coexist with different ways of thinking and living, but there are also critical Muslim voices who see fragmentation and weakening of unity in it.[194]

Clearly distinguishable from the religion of Islam is Islamic fundamentalism, also called Islamism. Islamic fundamentalism shares with other fundamentalisms the

---

[189] cf. Lipka & Hackett (2017), online: <http://www.pewresearch.org/fact-tank/2017/04/06/why-muslims-are-the-worlds-fastest-growing-religious-group/>

[190] cf. Ohlig & Stölting (2000), p. 14

[191] cf. N.N., online: <https://www.remid.de/archiv-mit-dokumentationsstelle/>

[192] cf. Leggewie (2002), p. 13

[193] cf. Krämer (2002), pp. 18–25

[194] cf. *ibid.*, p. 18

rejection of western modernity and its central elements such as individualization, Pluralism, human rights, democracy or secularization. but in contrast to these the Islamic fundamentalism affirms scientific and technical knowledge and their use.

Although Islamism is a heterogeneous phenomenon in the Islamic world, as well as Islam itself,[195] their followers have one connected target: Islam have to be the basis and guideline of all thinking and acting. An *"Islamic order"* should emerge, in which religion, law and politics form a unity – private and public life exclusively must be based on Islamic Norms and values: The *"theocratical state"* is the goal. Simply said Muslims and Islamists can be distinguished by this connection or separation of the three points – religion, law and policy. As criteria of distinction between Islamists and Muslims, the literature also mentions the following criteria:[196]

- Rejection of the separation of religion and state
- Constitution of the state according to Islamic law, sharia, and solitary Sharia law
- Appealing to a "model Medina" as a model for the formation of the community
- an overarching perception of inner world and outer world (of Islamic World and non-Islamic world)
- Israel criticism and questioning the right to exist of Israel
- anti-Semitic attitude
- no gender equality and a defined role allocation for husband and wife
- fixation on a certain (conservative) interpretation of the Koran

There exist diverging scientific views whether the willingness to violence, terror and jihad are among the characteristic features of Islamism[197] or not[198].

---

[195] cf. Ghaussy (1989), pp. 83–100
[196] cf. Dehn (2006), online: <http://www.ezw-berlin.de/html/15_1129.php>
[197] cf. Mayer (2006), pp. 181–88
[198] cf. Dehn, *supra* note 197

9.1.2 Salafism

Salafists describe themselves as defenders of an original, unadulterated Islam and demand a theocracy with a definite interpretation of sharia according to an ultra-conservative interpretation of the Koran. Their call for a state based solely on Islamist law, in conjunction with its transnational organization, gives reason to see this group linked to jihadism.[199]

9.1.3 Jihadism

Often the term jihad is falsely translated as holy war - the real meaning of the phrase *"struggling"*, *"making an effort for something"* and *"striving for something"*. Jihad is an action principle that distinguishes between the *"bigger"* and the *"smaller"* jihad. The bigger Jihad is the fight against evil in one's own heart. The smaller jihad is the legal defense of Islam in every form. The definition of smaller jihad is thus a factor that makes this term the name of the *"holy war"* in the eyes of Islamists. Therefore, the definition of the defense case is an important aspect for the distinction of Islam as a peaceful religion and Islamism as political ideology.[200]

9.2 The Islamic State

9.2.1 History of the IS

The origins and logic of the IS evolves around the obsession of reinstating the Muslim Caliphate. Islamic political ideology evolves around the notion of having in place a *"Calipha"*, who is the head of state. In this regard, politically the end of World War I was a particularly difficult time period for the Muslim world. The very revered and celebrated institution of the Caliphate in the Muslim world was in demise with the abolishment of the Ottoman Caliphate in 1926. As a response, in Al-Azhar University in Egypt convened the *"Congress of the Caliphate"* in attempts to uphold the ideology of the Caliphate.[201] The Congress of the Caliphate drafted and passed two key resolutions regarding the Caliphate. The first resolution pertained to the Caliph and stated that he must be an individual who has the capability of defending Islam. The second resolution being more functional and

---

[199] cf. Rauf & Jokisch (2014), pp. 15–36

[200] cf. *ibid.*, 70f

[201] cf. Liebl (2009), p. 387

controversial in nature stated that - the Caliphate ca be installed through conquest with legitimizing the use of force and violence.[202] Liebl further remarks that

> "[...] there exists now in the Muslim world legitimate caliphate bloodlines; organizational and economic foundations; and potentially legal authority to restore the caliphate today. All that is needed is the will [...]".[203]

The resolve to institute an Islamic State can be encapsulated in three stabs of deviations from the Al-Qaeda organization in the form of discrepant factions from within. The former leader of Al-Qaeda, Osama Bin Laden, reportedly opposed such an establishment of an Islamic State on the reasoning that attempts to establish a state are too premature and will not cope due the lack of public support and will. Regardless of such reasoning, Abu Massab Al-Zaraqwi went ahead to create a potential Islamic State; a detached branch of Al-Qaeda in 2004; known as *"The Council for Mujahedeen"*. The nature of the off-shoot organization was a resistance movement which stood against the presence of USA in Iraq. The council accommodated many other similar organizations under its ambit which had similar aspirations. This council later evolved into the Islamic State of Iraq (ISI). Simultaneously, Abu Bakr Al-Bagdadi, also a then Al-Quaeda front-runner, in resistance to USA presence in Iraq, co-founded the *"Jamaat Jaysh Ahl al Sunnah Wa-al Jamaah"* (the Army of the Sunni People Group); an insurgent group which operated in Samarra, Diyala and Baghdad. Later in 2006, this organization assimilated into the Council for Mujahedeen. Eventually, Al- Bagdadi rose to the title of the ruler and leader of the ISI organization after the death of Al-Zaraqwi.[204]

Catalyzed by the political instability of the region and further complimented by a still growing military strength and resource, ISI soon expanded to the Islamic State of Iraq and Syria (ISIS). Ultimately, on June 29th,2014, IS declared itself *"the Caliphate"* - under the leadership of Bakr Al-Bagdadi.[205] Since then, the IS in Iraq and Syria has established itself as an organization that aspires to re-establish and re-institutionalize the Islamic caliphate system and the instalment of Sharia law. To meet these end, the IS began its operations in regions which had a Sunni majority in Iraq and Syria and then followed by an expansion into other areas. Be-

---

[202] cf. *ibid.,* p. 388

[203] *ibid.,* p. 388

[204] cf. Weiss & Hassan, *supra* note 33, p. 113

[205] cf. Stern & Berger, *supra* note 35, p. 46

cause of this expanding beyond Iraq and Syria within the Levant region the IS got its new name - Islamic State in Syria (ISIS) or Islamic State of the Levante (ISIL). It is currently present in Yemen, Libya, Sinai Peninsula (Egypt), Somalia, Nigeria and Pakistan.[206]

The IS is a relatively nascent organization, a quick tour down history lane reveals that Islamic political history is laced with several leaders and movements for whom reinstalling the Caliphate had been the major motif. However, even though these movements shared the common central theme of Islamic caliphate they varied scientifically, which hence begs the question of authenticity of religious revivalism.[207] It is futile to identify one reference point of Islamic fundamentalism as each movement is distinctive given its context, aims and specific historical narrative. Regardless, the first theorist of modern Islamic fundamentalism can be traced back to the Egyptian Hassan El Banna and Pakistani Abu al-Ala Mawdudi.[208] Mawdudi, elucidated upon the political notion of Islam by stating the *"al-Islam deen we dawla"*, meaning that Islam is a religion and a state, rather than just being established as a concept of merely a religion, *"iqamat el deen"*.[209] He encouraged the juxtaposition of religion and state as a means of rules and procedure for society.[210] The call for the instalment of the Sharia law, by the two thinkers can also be associated as a form of resistance to the western influence which was increasing in dominance at the time and threatened Islam.

Although the name *"Da'esh"*[211] is currently being used by politicians for the terrorist organization IS all over the world, for the sake of simplicity I used the term IS in this master thesis.

9.2.2 The political, social, historical and psychological logic of the IS

In addition to the theological motivation behind the establishment of the IS, many political, social, historical and psychological reasons reveal themselves. Socially, increasing population figures, complimented by decreasing levels of education and employment rationalized the establishment of a new state. Politically, the

---

[206] cf. McCants (2015), p. 140

[207] cf. Marty & Appleby (1994), p. 839

[208] cf. Delanty & Kumar (2006), p. 184

[209] cf. Marty & Appleby, *supra* note 208, p. 824

[210] cf. Mohomed (2014), p. 289

[211] It is an acronym for *„ad-daula al-islāmiyya fī l-'Irāq wa-š-Šām"* (Arabic expression for ISIL)

failure of the states to accommodate and unify various political thoughts and ideologies under one umbrella and rather suppress and oppress them into their own ideological framework nurtured fundamentalist ideologies. In the domain of the historical and psychological, the widespread use of violence, torture, mass killings, frequent incarcerations and long term civil war hewed an ambiance in which extremist ideologies flourished. This coupled with the theological understand that advocates for the establishment of the caliphate system as a religious duty all contributed as factors which led to the institution of the IS.

The underlining ideology that dictates the principles of a caliphate system is grounded in the representation and succession. In many Islamic religious interpretations, the calipha is at the very epicenter of the Islamic political ideological understanding, without which the very system of the Caliphate is futile and inapplicable. IS is also part of so called ideological bandwagon and harmonize to the notion that without a calipha, most of the sharia law is not applied. Some members of the IS specified that *"Islam has been re-established"* with the formation of the state.[212] Furthermore, this is coupled with the understanding that the caliph, be it Al-Bagdadi or Ibrahim, serves as the appointed leader of all the Muslims on earth, bestowed with the responsibility of carrying out Allah's will with the power vested in him by the spiritual authority. There are various criteria for being nominated as the caliph. Al-Bagdadi hails from the bloodline of the Quraysh tribe, which is the same tribe from which the prophet Mohammad emerges from.[213] Thus, the ideology of the Caliphate is not only a duty to be carried out, it is in fact a movement with a selected leader, with a clear justifiable noble vision.[214]

9.2.3 IS's ideological and theological inclinations

The IS adheres and borrows from the *"Wahhabbi School of thought"* in Islam. *"Wahhabism"* is a form of Salafi ideology, an ideological movement which is prevalent in Saudi Arabia[215] and has an ultra-puritanical bent to it (view also Appendix 11.1.2). The IS shares common grounds with concepts of *"Wahabism"* such as

---

[212] cf. Wood (2015), online: <https://www.theatlantic.com/magazine/archive/2015/03/what-isis-really-wants/384980/>

[213] cf. Atwan, Abdel, Bari (2015), online: <https://www.thecairoreview.com/essays/a-portrait-of-caliph-ibrahim/>

[214] cf. Ingram, *supra* note 100, p. 461

[215] cf. Commins (2006), p. 1f

"*Tawhid*" (worship of one god – Allah), "*Hijra*" (migrations), "*Da'wah*" (invitation to Islam) and "*Takfir*" (excommunication/infidelity). Enjoying state power to enforce their ideologies on the masses is a central theme in both movements.[216] The "*Wahhabi*" movement and the IS are also both obsessed with a pan-Islamism understanding of the Muslim world, where all Muslims unite and strive to expand beyond that confining notions of the modern state in attempts to spread their message across the world. To this end, the IS aspires to re-establish the Caliphate to unite divided Muslims[217] and regain the lost glory of the Muslims. Within these ends, the IS hopes to dominate the entire world.[218]

Spurting from Islamic apocalyptical prophecies, the IS and the "*Wahhabi school of thought*" apportion the world into two pieces: "*Dar al-Islam*" (house of Islam) and "*Dar al-Kufr*" (house of infidelity). Such a division of the world prompts the understanding within the two movements of having a monopoly over religious truth and have been bestowed with the responsibility of inviting the masses, by further building up on apocalyptic understands regarding the preparation for the end of days.[219] To this end, the very location of the IS in Syria is not a mere coincidence, it is the prophesied location where the ultimate last battle between right and wrong will take place. The IS views itself as the one unified army of Islam, which will defeat the prophesied eighty flags (infidel forces) in the final battle.[220]

In this regard, the utilization of extreme violence by the IS on and off the battlefield, is just to conquer territories through power, but is also to realize the prophecies mentioned in Islamic apocalyptical literature. Finally, the IS and the "*Wahhabi school*" adhere to the notion that the arrival of the "*Mahdi*",[221] will coincide with the breakdown of the political institutions in the Middle East. All these narratives regarding the apocalyptical understandings with in Islam, coupled with the instability of the Levante region, help propel the agenda of the IS forward.

---

[216] cf. Al-Ibrahim (2015), p. 410

[217] cf. *ibid.*, p. 412

[218] cf. Al-Tamimi, Aymenn, Jawad (2014), online: <http://www.aymennjawad.org/14363/the-dawn-of-the-islamic-state-of-iraq-and-ash-sham>

[219] cf. Ingram, *supra* note 100, p. 458f

[220] cf. McCants, *supra* note 207, p. 104

[221] *ibid.*, p. 4

9.2.4 IS in numbers and statistics

Statistics on the IS's activity's pay homage to the success of the IS's communication campaign. As of December 2015, estimates indicate that around 20.000 to 30.000 foreign fighters have travelled to Syria and Iraq between the years 2011 and 2014. For a comparative perspective, only 10.000 to 20.000 foreign fighters have been estimated to have travelled to Muslim lands between the years 1980 and 2010.[222] Thus, the current immigration of foreign fighters to Muslim lands is quoted as

> "[...] the largest mobilization of foreign fighters in Muslim majority countries since 1945 [...]".[223]

More worryingly, numbers indicate that as of June 2014 the numbers of foreign fighters who have migrated to support the IS's activities has doubled in merely 18 months.[224] An attraction of foreign fighters by the IS like this, is particularly disturbing as during this time the IS suffered from losses of over 12.800 km^2 of territory.[225] This is indicative of the notion that their propaganda is strongly effective notwithstanding the actual ground realities. Furthermore, simultaneously the home (Western) countries of the migrating foreign fighters experienced a sharp spike in home-grown terrorist plots and attacks, for example Australia observed one third of its terrorism related arrest since 2001 ensuing within a six-month period beginning in late 2014.[226] During the period of January 2011 and June 2015, home-grown terrorism plots in Western Nations uncovered that 30 out of 69 plots had some connection to the IS, with 26 of the 30 occurring between July 2014 and June 2015.

Moreover, the probability of IS linked stratagems to be implemented was estimated to be twice of those with no IS links. Aside from the fact that, most of the rogue

---

[222] cf. Ingram, *supra* note 100, p. 458

[223] Neumann (2015), online: <http://icsr.info/2015/01/foreign-fighter-total-syriairaq-now-exceeds-20000-surpasses-afghanistan-conflict-1980s/>

[224] cf. Barrett (2015), online: <http://soufangroup.com/wp-content/uploads/2015/12/TSG_ForeignF ightersUpdate3.pdf>

[225] cf. N.N. (2015), online: <http://news.ihsmarkit.com/press-release/aerospace-defense-security/isl amic-states-caliphate-shrinks-14-percent-2015>

[226] cf. Ingram, *supra* note 100, p. 458

individuals had even not met or communed directly with the IS agents.[227] Studies have indicated that the IS's proficient and striking multidimensional communication campaign plays an indispensable role in shaping the trend of IS enthused foreign fighters migrating from the West to support their agenda.[228]

9.2.5 IS media departments

The so called "official media departments" of the IS produce and disseminate propaganda products as mouthpieces for the organization, demonstrating IS's communication strategy and demonstrating its goals, strategy and tactics. The Federal Office for the Protection of the Constitution (BfV) counts on its website(pictures and descriptions extracted from the website of the BfV)[229]:

"Al-Furqan", the official main media office. It acts as an exclusive media office for the management level of IS. Messages from this media section often contain directional content for the organization.

"Al-Hayat Media Center", responsible for publications in languages other than Arabic. This media center communicates with the non-Arab public in terms of language and content. The quality and layout of this propaganda is reminiscent of Western film productions, computer games and glossy magazines.

---

[227] cf. Hegghammer & Nesser (2015), online:
<http://www.terrorismanalysts.com/pt/index.php/pot/ article/view/440/html>

[228] cf. Ingram, *supra* note 100, p. 459

[229] cf. BfV (2018), online:
<https://www.verfassungsschutz.de/de/aktuelles/schlaglicht/schlaglicht-2016-12-kommunikationsstrategie-des-is>

"Ajnad" produces audios in the form of religious edifices such as Koran recitations and Anashid (anthemic battle song, usually to glorify fight and fighters).

"Al-Bayan Radio", which is also available as internet radio.

The weekly newspaper *"al-Naba'"*, which mainly publishes reports of operations and infographics as well as reports on current events. Thus, in the 40th edition of "al-Naba '" on 26 July 2016, an alleged biography of the assassin of Ansbach (attack of 24 July 2016).

Other internet-based organizations, such as "Amaq", which are repeatedly referred to as the "speech-tube" in the Western media[230], are not described in this master's thesis.

9.2.6 Timeline "Rumiyah" – terrorist attacks in Europe

Here I will show a short self-made timeline. I put the publication date of the single issues of *"Rumiyah"* in relation to bigger assassinations throw Europe and Western oriented states in that time. I want to demonstrate that in fact there is the theoretical possibility that radicalized assassins have actually followed the portrayals, explanations of the procedures, loss of territory in Syria and calls for attacks.

---

[230] cf. Rossi (2016), online: <http://www.tagesschau.de/amaq-nachrichtenagentur-101.html>

Issue no. 1 September 05th 2016		September 17th 2016 – bombings in New York and New Jersey
Issue no. 2 October 04th 2016		October 16th 2016 – suicide bomber in Gaziantep October 16th 2016 – Assault to recapture Mosul begins October 16th 2016 – Dabiq captured by Turkish backed Syrian rebel forces
Issue no. 3 November 11th 2016		November 21st 2016 – knife attack in Amsterdam
Issue no. 4 December 07th 2016		December 21st 2016 – Berlin Christmas market attack
Issue no. 5 January 06th 2017		January 1st 2017 – Istanbul nightclub attack
Issue no. 6 February 04th 2017		
Issue no. 7 March 07th 2017		March 22nd 2017 – vehicle attack on a bridge near the center of London
Issue no. 8 April 04th 2017		April 3rd 2017 – suicide bomber in the St. Petersburg April 7th 2017 – vehicle attack in the city of Stockholm

Issue no. 9 May 04th 2017		May 22nd 2017 – suicide bomber during a pop concert in Manchester
Issue no. 10 June 17th 2017		June 3rd 2017 – vehicle attack on the London bridge in the city of London
Issue no. 11 July 13th 2017		July 14th 2017 – knife attack (German tourists) in Hurgada July 28th 2017 – knife attack in Hamburg
Issue no. 12 August 06th 2017		August 6th 2017 – knife attack in front of the Eiffel Tower in Paris August 17th 2017 – vehicle attack in Barcelona August 25th 2017 – knife attack in front of the Buckingham Palace in London
Issue no. 13 September 09th 2017		September 15th 2017 – knife attack in the subway of Paris September 15th 2017 – bombing in the subway of London September 30th 2017 – vehicle attack in Edonton

Figure 10: Timetable release date "Rumiyah" – terrorist attacks

9.3 Development of the police crime statistics

The following evaluation describes the development of politically motivated foreigner crime in Germany for the past 10 years. The development of cases in the police criminal statistics (PKS) – throughout Germany – is put in relation with the population. Afterwards these results are compared with the development of cases in the criminal-police reporting path of politically motivated foreigner crime (called PMAK). Before the results of this evaluation are presented, the content of the two databases will be shown briefly:

The PKS contains the number of illegal acts (included punishable attempts) become known to the police, the number of suspects identified and several other information about these cases, the victims and the suspects. Politically motivated crime, traffic offences, administrative offences, offences which are not part of police responsibility (e.g. financial and tax evasion) and criminal offenses – which are directly reported to the public prosecutor - are not included.[231]

Crimes committed by a political motivation (politically motivated crime) are recorded separately in the PMK. Starting from the motives for action and the circumstances, politically motivated acts are assigned to corresponding subject areas and sub-themes. Subsequently, the recognizable ideological background and causes of the crime are portrayed in a phenomenon area of a situation report.[232]

The PMAK (one of the subsets of the PMK) constitutes offences, considering the conditions of the offense and / or the findings about the offender, especially if the perpetrator's non-German background and fundamentalist attitude was the reason for the committed offences, particular if it is focused on: manipulation of relations and developments at home and abroad or the try of taking influence from abroad to relations and developments within the federal republic of Germany.

PMAK offences can be committed by Germans, too. In this context offences are documented, which are motivated by imported ideologies from foreign countries (e.g. Islamism or fundamentalism).[233] In this phenomenon area, however, a more delicate breakdown is statistically not possible. Before this background the pure overall development of the PKS and the PMAK is compared.

Databases for the following table and charts are PKS table 01[234] and the German Interior Ministry report about political motivated crime in Germany[235].

---

[231] cf. BKA (2018), online:
<https://www.bka.de/DE/AktuelleInformationen/StatistikenLagebilde
r/PolizeilicheKriminalstatistik/PKS2016/pks2016_node.html>

[232] cf. Deutscher Bundestag (2017), online:
<https://www.bundestag.de/blob/503858/029b5f6683ed
2807959d7e1c55853af0/antisemtismusbericht_bericht-data.pdf>

[233] cf. *ibid.*

[234] cf. BKA, *supra* note 232

[235] cf. BfV (2018), online:
<https://www.verfassungsschutz.de/de/oeffentlichkeitsarbeit/publikation
en/verfassungsschutzberichte>

Year	Population Germany	Crime cases complete	Frequency number complete	Frequency number index in %	PMAK cases complete	Frequency number PMAK	Frequency number index in %
2007	82.314.909	6.284.661	7.635	100,0%	902	1,096	100%
2008	82.217.818	6.114.128	7.437	97,4%	1.484	1,805	180%
2009	82.002.546	6.054.330	7.383	96,7%	966	1,178	118%
2010	81.802.211	5.933.278	7.253	95,0%	917	1,121	112%
2011	81.751.648	5.990.679	7.328	96,0%	1.010	1,235	124%
2012	81.844.037	5.997.040	7.327	96,0%	868	1,061	106%
2013	80.523.826	5.961.662	7.404	97,0%	874	1,085	109%
2014	80.767.884	6.082.064	7.530	98,6%	2.549	3,156	316%
2015	81.197.560	6.330.649	7.797	102,1%	2.025	2,494	249%
2016	82.175.246	6.372.526	7.755	101,6%	3.372	4,103	410%
2017	82.521.539	5.761.984	6.982	91,4 %	2.719	3,294	329 %

Figure 11: Comparison of figures from PKS table 01 and BMI report about political crime

The increase rate of PMAK can be seen better in the following charts than in the table above:

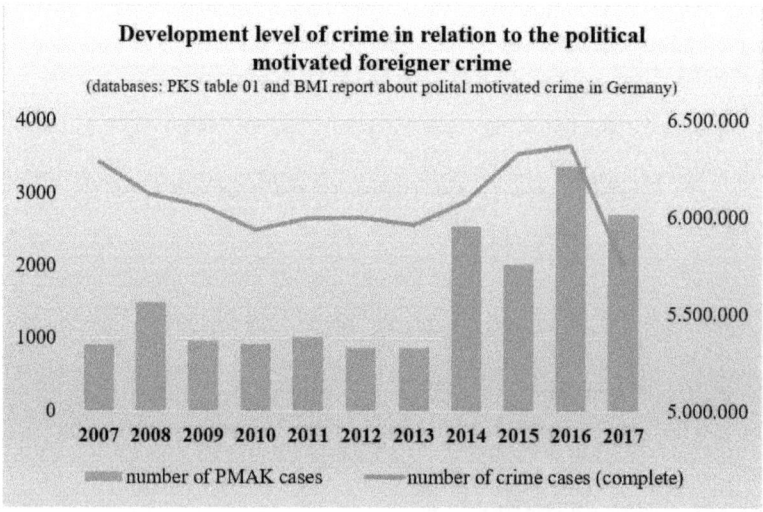

Figure 12: Development sum of incidents in relation to the political motivated foreigner crime

Looking at the pure number of cases, the reader can determine that the absolute number of criminal cases decreased from 2007 on, but it increased again from 2014 to a significant higher level, before it fell down last year.

The number of PMAK cases stayed at a constant level since 2007 – after 2013 it sharply increased and remains at a high level. A consideration of the pure case numbers would be misleading, because on the one hand the crime trends are not set in relation to the population and on the other hand the number of PMAK cases is a fraction of the total criminal cases. That's the reason why a comparison of the frequency numbers is essential.

The difference in development is best illustrated by an index comparison of the general frequency number and the PMAK frequency number (see chart below): Thus, the general frequency number remained at a constant level – whereas the frequency number of PMAK raised between 2007 and 2016 about 310 %.

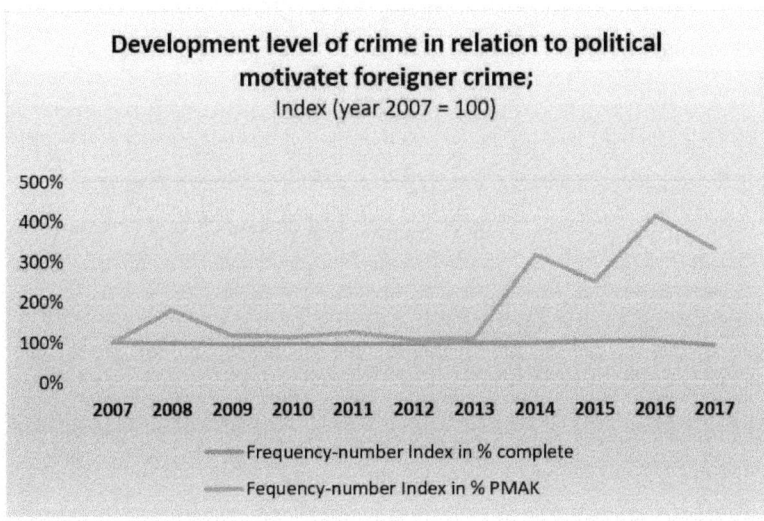

Figure 13: Development crime level in relation to political motivated foreigner crime level (index comparison)

9.4 Analysis – Results

9.4.1 Analysis category system

Content analysis category-system:

Upper category	Category	Sub category	Definition / code rule	Example from the text
Deprivation			Expressions of one's own, perceived victimhood in Western majority society and / or as a community of faith in the world; Representation of one's own actions as self-defense (contrast to category social relationship and affiliation]). Important role in the phase of cognitive opening.	"They carried on with their pacifist and even pro-democracy da'wah while Muslim woman around the world were being abused, vilified, imprisoned, and violated at the hands of the kuffar and their puppets." (issue 1; p 15)
Social relationship and affiliation	Superiority of IS		Representation and assertions of one's own power, the military strength of IS; Coding rule: also threats against the enemy	"The Americans faced a great massacre, to the extent that many of them were seen fleeing from the battle, hiding in Muslims' houses. At first, the mujahidin refrained from entering those homes for fear of harming the Muslims, but once they confirmed the presence of the American troops inside them, they found them hiding like cowards and began killing them as if they were beetles and flies, and all excellence and blessing belong to Allah." (issue 10; p. 9)

Upper category	Category	Sub category	Definition / code rule	Example from the text
	IS as Avant-gard		Members of the IS as chosen and representative of god, community of like-minded people, self-image as a kind of "avant-garde"	"As for the mujahidin in Allah's cause – and they are the elite of His creation, those of His slaves whom He has chosen to become martyrs and whom He subjects to favorable tests – then the death of their leaders and commanders who stormed ahead of them into battle, running head first into hardships for their religion, only increases their firmness and determination in fighting the enemies of Allah." (issue 1; p3.)
	Achievment of IS		Descriptions of successes of the group, military victories territorial expansion and membership growth	"Meanwhile, the soldiers of the Islamic State succeeded in damaging 4 Abrams tanks, destroying 16 hummers, [...] Additionally, several members of the Rafidi army and their militias were killed and wounded." (issue 1; p. 25)
	Social Security		Social security within the family or the material security with respect to one's own existence (home) or the income or food, as well as emphasis on equality and the idea of the community.	"[...] the amir of the Central Office for Investigating Grievances clarified the reason behind the office's establishment, and the role it plays in eliminating the injustices that might afflict both the subjects and soldiers of the Islamic State. [...]" (issue 1; p. 10)

Upper category	Category	Sub category	Definition / code rule	Example from the text
Orientation and meaningfulness	Concept of the enemy		Oppositions and the division of the world into pairs of opposites: division into good and evil, false faith - true faith; Coding rule: also, the explicit naming of the enemies, always involves assessment, coding outgoing from the subject of the sentence and whereby this is primarily characterized	
		Wrong religion	All the statements concerning those individuals and groups who adhere to the wrong religion, which are often understood as majority-minded. Individuals and groups are characterized by their belonging to a false religion (community).	"An individual is not saved form the filth and impurity of shirk and its people as long as he does not disbelieve in the tawaghit of his era, [...] Also included is the "Murtadd Brotherhood" group and its parties, factions and sister organizations, [...]" (issue 1; p. 6)
		The west and allies	Western nation states, including Russia, Japan and their cooperation partners (Israel, Arab states, Assad regime, "Western" concepts like nationalism, secularism)	"The old colonialism was but a front for the Crusaders, just as it is today a front for the Jews and Christians. Indeed, the "Caesar of Rome" Bush has declared multiple times that, "It is a Crusade!"" (issue 2; p.19)

Upper category	Category	Sub category	Definition / code rule	Example from the text
		Other jihadist groups	Differentiation to other jihadist groups that have not submitted or affiliated to IS, for example Al Qaeda, al-Nusra	"Fighting the Islamic State ultimately became a joint project between the Taliban movement and the nations of kufr, who were terrified by the presence of the Islamic State on their borders, just as its presence terrified the United States of America, which occupies Afghanistan." (issue 10; p. 42f)
	Clear rules		Prescriptions of behavioral statements that determine everyday life and point the way forward; concrete ideas about behavior in jihad, everyday life and co.; punishments due to misconduct, too	"This form of jihad (the jihad through du'a) is more emphasized in the case of those for whom Allah exempted from fighting for His cause, such as woman, the ill, the disabled, and the imprisoned. They should all make du'a for the mujahidin, for indeed, when Allah excused the exempted, [...]" (issue 3; p. 33)
	Supposed noble targets		Supposedly higher or holy goal of the group	"We ask Allah to strengthen the mujahidin of the Islamic State, so they may liberate Makkah and Madinah from the tawaghit of Al Salul - may Allah disgrace them - and to bless us with hajj and 'umrah in the shade of the Shari'ah." (issue 1; p. 33)

Upper category	Category	Sub category	Definition / code rule	Example from the text
	Adventure and borderline experience		Promoting participation in the struggle and in the adventurous life of the IS	This category has been included in the analysis for comparability with the analysis work about the "Dabiq" magazine from the secondary literature. In my analysis, no sense units could be identified that would have been subsumed under this purely (if then this category was marginalized, but the main context was different).
	Delimitation to the majority		Turning away from norms and behaviors of the majority society or the "wrong Muslims"	"Thus, a person cannot be a Muslim except by adhering to Islam in both of these aspects, so whoever doesn't submit to Allah – such as one who abandons all actions or forcefully resists some of the manifest, mutawatir rulings – is nothing but a kafir, and whoever isn't exclusively for Allah – such as one who worships the prophets and the righteous, whether blindly following others or having misunderstandings – is nothing but a mushrik, even if he prays, fasts, and claims that he is a Muslim." (issue 1; p. 5)

Upper category	Category	Sub category	Definition / code rule	Example from the text
	Call for change and action		Direct and indirect call for active action, emigration to the caliphate, battle of jihad and annihilation of opponents as well as call for terrorist acts in Western countries. Coding rules: direct addressing, imperatives in the second person singular and plural, also "should" constructions	"Kill them on the streets of Brunswick, Broadmeadows, Bankstown, and Bondi. Kill them at the MCG, the SCG, the Opera House, and even in their backyards. Stab them, shoot them, poison them, and run them down with your vehicles." (issue 1; p. 17f)

Figure 14: Content analysis category system

Layout analysis category -system:

Category – Keyword for content	Definition – code rule	Example from the text
Glorify CV	This keyword includes glorifying CV, from "heroes" of the IS (also showing CV of suicide assassins).	"Among the Believers Are Men Abu Mansur al-Muhajir" (issue 1, p.14ff)
History	Representation of historical events according to tradition (Hadith or Koran). Also the representation of historical events and their interpretation from the point of view of the worldview of the IS are coded here.	"Sultan Mahmud Al-Ghaznawi" (issue 3, p.36ff)
Interview	Text in the form of an interview in direct speech. The representation takes place in question and answer (with name of the respective speaking one).	"Interview with the Amir of the Central office for investigating grievances" (issue 1, p.10ff)
Propaganda Promotion	Direct advertising for the download of videos, apps, etc. which are distributed by the IS or a related organization in the world wide web.	"Selected 10 Videos From The Wilayat Of The Islamic State" (issue 1, p.9)
Religion	Reports with a religious background. These include, on the one hand, the theological justification for different behaviors and the theological background to the construction of the IS. Also included are reports that show a theological delineation from the moderate currents of Islam.	"The Religion of Islam And the Jama'ah of the Muslims" (issue 2, p. 14ff)
Report	This keyword was given for reports from everyday life within the IS, as well as, for example, the presentation of political events outside the IS. It has also been used to encode texts that disseminate "general knowledge" in the sense of the ideology of the IS.	"Stand and Die Upon That for Which Your Brothers Died" (issue1, p. 2f)

Speech	The summary or transcribed presentation of speeches that have been made - by clergy or responsible persons of the IS.	"This is what Allah and his Messenger promised us" (issue 3, p.4ff)
Successes	Under this keyword representations of success are subsumed. The presentation can take the form of a text or a graphic.	"Military and Covert Operations" (issue 4, 34ff)
Terror Tactics	This Keyword includes articles, that describe terror tactics and thus animate for imitation (approach, advantages, disadvantages ...).	"Just Terror Tactics" (issue 1, p. 12f)
Title	This keyword contains the title page, back cover, and table of contents (if the issue has it).	Title, back cover – every issue, additionally the table of content started in issue 7 (The representation of the anchor example was omitted in this case.)

Figure 15: Layout analysis category system

9.4.2 Analysis datasheets in detail

The summary tables of the evaluation are shown below. The individual evaluation forms for the respective issues are stored on the data carrier enclosed with the master thesis.

9.4.3 Table of content – Datasheets

- Results of the content analysis work (issue no. 1 – 13) – in numbers
- Results of the content analysis work (issue no. 1 – 13) – in percent
- Result of the layout analysis work (issue no. 1 – 13) – keyword content in summary
- Results of the layout analysis work (issue no. 1 – 13) – keyword content in pages
- Results of the layout analysis work (issue no. 1 – 13) – pictures in context of keywords

Code rules	Issue No. 1	Issue No. 2	Issue No. 3	Issue No. 4	Issue No. 5	Issue No. 6	Issue No. 7	Issue No. 8	Issue No. 9	Issue No. 10	Issue No. 11	Issue No. 12	Issue No. 13	Σ total	Σ total in %
Deprivation	4	5	3	3	4	4	11	2	11	5	4	11	6	73	1,85%
Social Relationship and Affiliation														865	21,96%
Superiority of IS	2	9	16	15	4	15	3	6	30	18	16	20	13	167	4,24%
IS as Avantgard	6	26	14	16	10	5	11	11	19	9	19	9	10	165	4,19%
Achievement of IS	42	33	26	41	60	55	31	24	32	46	40	47	49	526	13,35%
Social Security	2	2	2	1	0	0	0	0	0	0	0	0	0	7	0,18%
Orientation and Meaningfulness														1389	35,26%
Clear rules	19	6	20	9	18	19	19	17	33	6	40	42	16	264	6,70%
Concept of the enemy														472	11,98%
Wrong religion	16	15	24	13	50	9	7	15	25	12	9	14	11	220	5,59%
The West and Allies	2	17	23	27	20	33	10	7	24	19	17	25	13	237	6,02%
Other jihadist groups	1	2	1	0	0	0	1	1	0	7	0	0	2	15	0,38%
Supposed noble targets	6	2	15	24	23	30	10	13	33	8	14	15	17	210	5,33%
Adventure and borderline experience	0	0	0	0	0	0	0	0	0	0	0	0	0	0	0,00%
Delimitation to the majority	21	20	23	22	22	9	43	26	20	9	17	14	42	288	7,31%
Call for change and action	14	11	11	13	20	9	6	3	19	5	32	1	11	155	3,94%
Uncoded Sense Units	120	111	167	89	127	77	57	130	154	115	198	173	94	1612	40,92%
Σ total	255	259	345	273	358	265	209	255	400	259	406	371	284	3939	100,0%

Figure 16: Content analysis results – in numbers

123

Code rules	Issue No. 1	Issue No. 2	Issue No. 3	Issue No. 4	Issue No. 5	Issue No. 6	Issue No. 7	Issue No. 8	Issue No. 9	Issue No. 10	Issue No. 11	Issue No. 12	Issue No. 13
Deprivation	1,6%	1,9%	0,9%	1,1%	1,1%	1,5%	5,3%	0,8%	2,8%	1,9%	1,0%	3,0%	2,1%
Social Relationship and Affiliation													
Superiority of IS	0,8%	3,5%	4,6%	5,5%	1,1%	5,7%	1,4%	2,4%	7,5%	6,9%	3,9%	5,4%	4,6%
IS as Avantgard	2,4%	10,0%	4,1%	3,9%	2,8%	1,9%	5,3%	4,3%	4,8%	3,5%	4,7%	2,4%	3,5%
Achievement of IS	16,5%	12,7%	7,5%	15,0%	16,8%	20,8%	14,8%	9,4%	8,0%	17,8%	9,9%	12,7%	17,3%
Social Security	0,8%	0,8%	0,6%	0,4%	0,0%	0,0%	0,0%	0,0%	0,0%	0,0%	0,0%	0,0%	0,0%
Orientation and Meaningfulness													
Clear rules	7,5%	2,3%	5,8%	3,3%	5,0%	7,2%	9,1%	6,7%	8,3%	2,3%	9,9%	11,3%	5,6%
Concept of the enemy — wrong religion	6,3%	5,8%	7,0%	4,8%	14,0%	3,4%	3,3%	3,9%	6,3%	4,6%	2,2%	3,8%	3,9%
the west and allies	0,8%	6,6%	6,7%	9,9%	5,6%	12,5%	4,8%	2,7%	6,0%	7,3%	4,2%	6,7%	4,6%
other jihadist groups	0,4%	0,8%	0,3%	0,0%	0,0%	0,0%	0,5%	0,4%	0,0%	2,7%	0,0%	0,0%	0,7%
Supposed noble targets	2,4%	0,8%	4,3%	8,8%	6,4%	11,3%	4,8%	5,1%	8,3%	3,1%	3,4%	4,0%	6,0%
Adventure and borderline experience	0,0%	0,0%	0,0%	0,0%	0,0%	0,0%	0,0%	0,0%	0,0%	0,0%	0,0%	0,0%	0,0%
Delimitation to the majority	8,2%	7,7%	6,7%	8,1%	6,1%	3,4%	20,6%	10,2%	5,0%	3,5%	4,2%	3,8%	14,8%
Call for change and action	5,5%	4,2%	3,2%	4,8%	5,6%	3,4%	2,9%	1,2%	4,8%	1,9%	7,9%	0,3%	3,9%
Uncoded Sense Units	47,1%	42,9%	48,4%	32,6%	35,5%	29,1%	27,3%	51,0%	38,5%	44,4%	48,8%	46,6%	33,1%

Figure 17: Content analysis results – in percent

content with Keyword	Issue No. 1	Issue No. 2	Issue No. 3	Issue No. 4	Issue No. 5	Issue No. 6	Issue No. 7	Issue No. 8	Issue No. 9	Issue No. 10	Issue No. 11	Issue No. 12	Issue No. 13	Σ per keyword
glorify CV	2	0	2	0	0	0	0	1	0	1	1	0	0	7
history	0	0	1	1	1	1	1	0	0	1	0	0	0	6
religion	6	4	7	6	4	5	9	9	6	5	2	3	4	70
report	1	6	3	5	7	6	2	3	1	4	5	6	4	53
speech	0	0	1	1	0	0	0	0	1	0	1	0	0	4
successes	2	4	2	6	4	3	2	3	2	1	3	3	3	38
terror tactics	1	1	1	1	1	0	0	0	2	0	0	0	0	7
title	2	2	2	2	2	2	3	3	3	3	3	3	3	33
propaganda promotion	1	2	0	1	0	2	2	2	2	3	2	2	4	23
interview	1	0	0	1	1	1	0	0	1	1	0	1	0	7
Σ content per issue	16	19	19	24	20	20	19	21	18	19	17	18	18	248
Pages per issue	38	38	46	40	44	44	38	48	58	46	60	46	44	
ratio pages Σ content	2,4	2,0	2,4	1,7	2,2	2,2	2,0	2,3	3,2	2,4	3,5	2,6	2,4	

Figure 18: Layout analysis results – content with keyword

pages with Keyword content	Issue No. 1	Issue No. 2	Issue No. 3	Issue No. 4	Issue No. 5	Issue No. 6	Issue No. 7	Issue No. 8	Issue No. 9	Issue No. 10	Issue No. 11	Issue No. 12	Issue No. 13	Σ
glorify CV	5	0	3	0	0	0	0	6	0	3	9	0	0	26
history	0	0	4	2.5	4	4	4	0	0	6	0	0	0	24.5
religion	16	8	15	10	5	11	19	25	21	11	7	5	15	168
report	2	18	9	7	17	14	6	7	7	11	27	27	15	167
speech	0	0	6	4	0	0	0	0	10	0	6	0	0	26
successes	6	6	4	9	9	6	4	5	4	3	6	5	7	74
terror tactics	3	2	3	1	3	0	0	0	7	0	0	0	0	19
title	2	2	2	2	2	2	3	3	3	3	3	3	3	33
propaganda promotion	1	2	0	0.5	0	2	2	2	2	3	2	2	4	22.5
interview	3	0	0	4	4	5	0	0	4	6	0	4	0	30
Σ pages	38	38	46	40	44	44	38	48	58	46	60	46	44	590

Figure 19: Layout analysis results – Keyword content in pages

pictures in content with Keyword	Issue No. 1	Issue No. 2	Issue No. 3	Issue No. 4	Issue No. 5	Issue No. 6	Issue No. 7	Issue No. 8	Issue No. 9	Issue No. 10	Issue No. 11	Issue No. 12	Issue No. 13	Σ per keyword
glorify CV	5	0	1	0	0	0	0	7	0	3	5	0	0	21
history	0	0	2	1	1	4	3	0	0	6	0	0	0	17
religion	11	5	8	5	3	9	14	26	20	10	6	3	9	129
report	3	11	7	8	14	12	5	6	4	7	17	17	9	120
speech	0	0	5	3	0	0	0	0	6	0	3	0	0	17
successes	9	6	4	10	9	6	5	5	4	3	6	9	6	82
terror tactics	1	1	4	3	2	0	0	0	13	0	0	0	0	24
title	2	2	2	2	2	2	7	6	6	5	5	5	5	51
propaganda promotion	10	11	0	5	0	11	5	5	5	6	5	5	10	78
interview	1	0	0	1	3	3	3	0	3	5	0	4	0	23
Σ pictures per issue	42	36	33	38	34	47	42	55	61	45	47	43	39	562
Pages per issue	38	38	46	40	44	44	38	48	58	46	60	46	44	
frequency per 100 pages	110,5	94,74	71,74	95	77,3	106,818	110,526	114,583	105,172	97,8261	78,3333	93,4783	88,6364	

Figure 20: Layout analysis results – pictures in context of keywords

9.4.4 Layout "Operations" – "Military and Covert Operations"

Particularly striking in the analysis work was the change in the background image in the ongoing series of articles "*Operations*" (later "*military and covert Operations*"), in which the successes of the IS were presented. Especially this series with a fixed place in each issue has a kind of recognition value and nevertheless, a change was carried out here:

Issue no. 1 and 2

Issue no. 3 – 7

Issue no. 8 and 9

Issue no. 10 - 13

9.4.5 Comparison analysis results "Dabiq" vs"Rumiyah"

To achieve comparable data's, the final results of the content analyzes of Kiefer et. al.[236] and mine are juxtaposed:

Code rules	"Dabiq" Σ total in %	"Rumiyah" Σ total in %
Deprivation	6,77%	1,85%
Social Relationship and Affiliation	18,30%	21,96%
Superiority of IS	3,53%	4,24%
IS as Avantgard	5,59%	4,19%
Achievment of IS	6,41%	13,35%
Social Security	2,77%	0,18%
Orientation and Meaningfulness	33,85%	35,26%
Clear rules	10,01%	6,70%
Concept of the enemy	16,33%	11,98%
Wrong religion	3,46%	5,59%
The West and Allies	6,75%	6,02%
Other jhadist groups	6,13%	0,38%
Supposed noble targets	1,33%	5,33%
Adventure and borderline experience	2,75%	0,00%
Delimitation to the majority	0,64%	7,31%
Call for change and action	2,79%	3,94%
Uncoded Sense Units	41,09%	40,92%
	100,00%	100,00%

Figure 21: Detail comparison analyiss results "Dabiq" vs. "Rumiyah"

---

[236] Kiefer et al., *supra* note 26

Lightning Source UK Ltd.
Milton Keynes UK
UKHW041025040822
406842UK00002B/325